Dr. Patel presents a American society. The thought-provoking topics offer a basis for discussions and in-depth analysis of modern culture.

- Judith Toscano RN. MSN Clinical System Analyst

I much appreciate how Dr. Patel unpacks her insightful, multinational approach and how it helps her reader gain a bigger picture view on the issues plaguing our collective society today. These are important topics that everyone needs to gain perspective on and to truly think about; I find this work to be timely, educational, and thought provoking.

- Jenifer M Brand, CMRP, Engineering Development Laboratory Manager

Dr. Patel takes you on a journey exploring the problems exhibited in American families today while offering a historical perspective and positive solutions for change. Her analysis of the workplace provides a look back at the widespread awakening of sexual abuse, discrimination, and the associated legal ramifications. Dr. Patel's sincere interest in analyzing the current, most severe sociological problems in the United States is to bring about change for a more compassionate, intelligent, and forward-thinking society. She attacked every problem with rigorous analysis, and most notably, offered recommendations. Dr. Patel is challenging all of us to reach for a higher standard of civility, morality, and responsibility to ourselves, our families, and our fellow citizens.

- Arthur D. Gottlieb, Retired Queensbury Middle School Principal, Queensbury, New York

US Unhinged delves into relevant challenges facing society today. Instead of turning to fear tactics, Dr. Patel turns to pragmatism and provides a language for important conversations; understanding how we got here and how we get out. Dr. Patel offers a dialogue rich in research and clinical experience.

- Catherine Kozen, Director Marketing & mom of 2

Dr. Patel's autobiography and perspective of our current American society illustrates and embodies the New American Dream. She is an immigrant from the third world; a woman of color who has faced and overcome immense challenges. Yet has maintained her levelheaded and fair-minded approach to life. For both the young and old, her ideas are a roadmap to acquire skills and achieve a mindset to face and overcome the challenges of our society.

- Paul Miller, Retired teacher

This book is wonderfully insightful, enlightening, frightening, and very sad in places. It has relevance today as it addresses many subjects from a professional, rather than a politically biased, individual's viewpoints. Everyone would benefit from reading it but especially parents. As a grandmother, all parts relating to children resonated with me. As I read the book, I found myself wishing my son and his wife were reading along with me. I gained insight and knowledge with a better understanding of what is happening in our country today. This is a very good book that hopefully, will reach many, many readers.

- Nancy Bray

I found US Unhinged engrossing. This book has so much relevance today. It doesn't matter how talented or rich you believe you are. It's how you treat people. Integrity is everything. I have benefitted greatly from reading this book. I am hoping to be more tolerant and respectful with my daughter and 17-year-old granddaughter, who was adopted from China at the age of 18 months and has a lot of problems. The book made me realize that your life is shaped by the decisions you make and have made, not by the ones you didn't. We all need to adopt a better understanding of people and their problems and appreciate our differences.

- Angela Paporello

I loved it! This is a book I would keep in my night table by my bed. The chapters are self-contained, and it is not necessary to read them in order. I was definitely challenged but felt I agree or have a similar belief system as the author, Dr. Patel. I felt the section on loneliness is very appropriate at this time with social distancing and self-quarantine during the pandemic.

- Gloria Ragonetti

Us UNHINGED

Book-1

Understanding your inner turmoil and how to make peace with yourself.

Then work to improve your personal and community relationships to heal our wounded nation.

Dr. Shila Patel, M.D.

Paperback ISBN: 978-1-7377849-3-7
Ebook ISBN: 978-1-7377849-4-4

Printed on acid-free paper.

Us Unhinged is printed in Times New Roman.

Library of Congress Cataloguing in Publication Data
Patel, M.D., Dr. Shila
Us Unhinged: Book-1 by Dr. Shila Patel, M.D.
Library of Congress Control Number: 2021919793

Dedicated to my Parents

They set a wonderful example and instilled within me
to have compassion for others and improve their lives.

Disclaimer

This book details the author's personal experiences with and opinions about societal problems, relationships, and parenting. The author is not currently a healthcare provider.

The author and publisher are providing this book and its contents on an "as is" basis and make no representations or warranties of any kind with respect to this book or its contents. The author and publisher disclaim all such representations and warranties, including for example warranties of healthcare for a particular purpose. In addition, the author and publisher do not represent or warrant that the information accessible via this book is accurate, complete or current.

The statements made about services have not been evaluated. They are not intended to diagnose, treat, cure, or prevent any condition or disease. Please consult with your own physician or healthcare specialist regarding the suggestions and recommendations made in this book.

Except as specifically stated in this book, neither the author or publisher, nor any authors, contributors, or other representatives will be liable for damages arising out of or in connection with the use of this book. This is a comprehensive limitation of liability that applies to all damages of any kind, including (without limitation) compensatory; direct, indirect, or consequential damages; loss of data, income or profit; loss of or damage to property and claims of third parties.

You understand that this book is not intended as a substitute for consultation with a licensed healthcare practitioner, such as your physician. Before you begin any healthcare program, or change your lifestyle in any way, you will consult your physician or other licensed healthcare practitioner to ensure that you are in good health and that the examples contained in this book will not harm you.

This book provides content related to topics of physical and/or mental health issues. As such, use of this book implies your acceptance of this disclaimer.

Chapter Summaries

Part 1 – Personal Journey

A Personal Journey

What is it that defines us and gives meaning to our existence? My journey began when my father decided to leave India at a young age. Our family has lived on four continents, from India to Africa, then to Great Britain, and finally to Florida in the United States. Experiences from growing up in the Eastern Indian culture and working professionally in the Western world have defined me as the woman I am today.

Introduction

Can we, as Americans, examine the ills that exist today and work together to create a healthier, more compassionate society for tomorrow's citizens? This analysis refers to all people, from the youngest to the oldest, promoting discipline, education, work ethic, family support, physical and mental health care for all, and respect for all human rights. This book is a sociological study of our American society today. It presents a discussion in understanding what has happened in our culture. Why have these beliefs and events transpired? How do we move forward to a more informed, compassionate, and disciplined society?

Part 2 - Enough is Enough - Get Over It

Sexual Abuse and Molestation

When does sexual "banter" get out of control? How do victims deal with abuse and molestation? How have the church and society dealt with emotionally laden issues? Well-known athletes, celebrities, and medical professionals have been affected. What changes in behavior and thought processes can we anticipate for the future?

The #MeToo Movement

Why was this movement started? What are the changes and resulting consequences that have occurred? Has enough light been shed on this issue to make permanent changes in the way men and women respect each other?

Men Accused of Sexual Misconduct

A review of judicial cases related to the sexual misconduct of men, including prominent men who have also made contributions to society, and other individuals, when charged, had a long history of sexually abusive behaviors towards women in their professions.

Part 3- Moving Forward

An Historical Perspective

Differences in the way males and females have been treated in ancient Christianity, Asian Indian cultures, China, Japan, and Egypt are explored. Issues are addressed to provide perspective, and an analysis of what to expect in the future, regarding male/female relationships.

The Yin and the Yang

Understanding the relationship between males and females from older traditions and how these values have served humanity well over the centuries are explored. Forward movement is usually positive but forgetting the past can have devastating consequences.

Sexual Behaviors and Why They Bond Men and Women Friends with Benefits
What is the purpose of sexual behaviors and what are some of the benefits of sexual activities? What changes are occurring in society regarding sexual behaviors?

Hope for Women and Society
There are a lot of positive changes that have come about in our lifetime. Let us focus on them and foster these changes. We cannot let a few misguided individuals detract us. There is a lot of hope that things can get better for everyone if we get past the distorted thinking and anger.

Last Thoughts to Ponder
Included are some personal issues highlighting some topics discussed throughout the book and how they affected my life. It is a challenge to move forward positively, rather than focus on negative aspects of life that leave humans feeling hopeless and pessimistic.

Acknowledgements

Us UNHINGED

Book-1

Table of Contents

Part 1

Personal Journey

A Personal Journey

My family history is no different from that of millions of others who decided to immigrate to the United States of America. Our journey was not a simple one, from India to Kenya, East Africa to Zambia, to Great Britain in Europe and then finally, to the state of Florida in America. Our story began when my father, Chhotubhai, known as C.N. all his life, was born in Pardi-Nogama, India, a small village of twenty-five houses in 1929. His name was shortened because non-Indians had difficulty pronouncing it correctly. In that same year, Jawaharlal Nehru was president of the Indian National Congress. Nehru called for complete independence from the British Raj, British rule.[1] In 1942, at the age of thirteen years, my father attended the congressional convention with his father, where Mahatma Gandhi delivered his "Quit India Speech." Gandhi made this speech to foster support for a resolution, whereby the British would quit, leave India after almost two hundred years of rule. Gandhi stated that he believed "in the history of the world, there has not been a more genuine democratic struggle for freedom than ours."[2] Other famous leaders in attendance on that momentous day, August 8, 1942, were Jawaharlal Nehru, Sardar Vallabhbhai, and many other renowned congressional members.[3]

The following year, my father's mother passed away. He moved in with his older sister who resided in a large city. During this time in India, Gandhi and his supporters pushed through their policy of non-violence, civil disobedience, and other campaigns to free India. My father focused on his studies and graduated from high school in 1947. It was an extraordinary year. Finally, after a tumultuous struggle, the Parliament of the United Kingdom passed the Indian Independence Act of 1947. British India was partitioned into two independent states of India and Pakistan. [4]

During this period, my father's older brother had already left India and settled in Kenya, East Africa. He sent my father a Kenyan work permit. As British subjects, Indians were able to leave India and settle in British colonies. My father was determined to leave India and secured a British passport. Less than a month after India became an independent nation on August 15, 1947, my father demonstrated outstanding courage. He left India with a friend and set sail for East Africa to join his brother. He was eighteen years old with twelve dollars in his pocket. The two friends traversed the ocean in the Amra steamer ship, which provided basic transportation and accommodations between India and Kenya. Their journey lasted twelve days, and they arrived in Mombasa, on the eastern shores of Kenya, East Africa.

My father had an amazing sense of adventure to take such an arduous journey at this time. This was before the time of cell phones, internet, GPS and even the land lines were very limited in Africa. He was not familiar with the geography of the world nor had knowledge about the available methods of transportation for travel. He had the will to complete the journey at a very young age. Back then, he understood that this was his chance to get out of extreme poverty. If he stayed in India, he would have been competing for employment with about 200 million other people. Somehow, he made his way over from a coastal port to Nakuru, in the Rift Valley of Kenya. His older brother was living and working there. Initially, my father began working with his brother in a store, in addition to taking some courses in bookkeeping. He felt it was his responsibility to bring his younger brother to Kenya and support his father financially, who still resided in India.

In 1942, my mother, Usha, left India at the age of eight years with her mother to join her father, in Jinja, Uganda, another British colony in East Africa. They had also crossed the ocean in the Karanja steamer between Mumbai and Mombasa. My mother remembers how seasick my grandmother was during the eight-day journey. Her only memory of this trip was holding my grandmother's head as she continued to throw up. She was unable to keep any food down. My mother was trying to comfort her. After the arduous journey, the two of them boarded a train to Jinja. My mother grew up in Uganda. My grandfather had a retail fabric business; he sold clothing material to local Africans. My grandparents lived in the back of the store. As a young child, I remember visiting them often with my mother and sisters during our December school vacation every year. I have very fond memories of sitting with my grandfather for hours, listening to the news and Indian songs on the radio. He enjoyed giving us small bananas and peeled apples to eat. The women were always busy in the kitchen: cooking, grinding lentils, preparing flour in stone mills, and stocking up on food supplies for the year.

The distance from Nakuru, Kenya to Jinja, Uganda, is over two hundred miles. Through an arranged marriage by relatives, my parents met. My father agreed to marry my mother only after she completed high school. She was sixteen years old, and he was twenty-two years old. Once my mother graduated, they married, and within a year my twin sisters were born. My mother recalls that at that time health services were just about non- existent. Together the twins weighed six pounds at birth. They were brought home in two shoe boxes. There was no NICU (Neonatal Intensive Care Unit) in those days; amazingly, my sisters survived. Three years later, I was born at home, delivered by a midwife. At a young age of twenty-one, she learned how to cook, sew, care for us, and became an excellent homemaker.

As far as gender roles, there was a clear distinction between my father's and mother's responsibilities. He provided for the immediate family's financial needs and shared the burdens of the extended family. My mother's role focused on raising the children and housekeeping. Growing up as children, we were free to roam and visit other relatives and families in the neighborhood. All family members participated in raising the children.

We lived in Nakuru until I was three years old. At that time, my father decided to move to Nairobi, the capital of Kenya. There were more job opportunities in the city. My father worked three jobs and attended evening accounting classes. He aspired to study and work as a physician, but there was no family money, available educational grants, or scholarships in those days. He settled into a profession where he excelled, working with numbers and accounting. At the beginning of our life in the capital, conditions were challenging. There was no running hot water or modern conveniences like a washing machine and other household appliances. Every morning my mother woke up early to begin her household chores. She lit coal fires to heat water for baths, washed clothes by hand, and mopped the floors with rags.

Both my parents struggled to make a better life for my sisters and me. Looking back at this part of my life, my parents were my mentors for work ethics They worked long hours and I have the tenacity to do the same to achieve my goals. I have little tolerance for people who complain and try to get away with minimal effort, producing mediocre work.

Despite working extremely hard, my father found the time to help us with our homework. As children, my mother did not permit us in the kitchen, where she prepared meals on open coal fires. My parents enjoyed participating in family activities. Our favorite past time was walking down the streets, "window shopping". We would look and admire the pretty things for sale but did not have to buy them. From an early age, we were taught that we could not get everything we wanted or be jealous of what others had. Instead, during our outings, we received a delicious treat of roasted corn or cassava chips, prepared by the locals to be sold to the pedestrians strolling by their stands. The aromas of the grilled vegetables filled the air. To this day, I enjoy corn, yuca or even peas in the pod roasted on an open fire. We used to go on picnics in the park with other families and visit the surrounding natural sights in Kenya. My parents had a great sense of adventure. We traveled throughout Africa even when African tribes were still throwing spears at passing cars, driving on dirt roads. Thankfully, we never suffered any injuries. On occasions, we would see lions lounging or walking along the roadway.

My parents left us girls with other family members and friends when they took some overseas trips. At an early age of five or six years, I remember being in bed with my sister and a young man in his twenties. He was kissing us, and I felt very uncomfortable. Even at that age, I understood that what he was doing was not right. We were fortunate that he did not take advantage of us sexually. This event was never addressed with my parents on their return or ever. I was not traumatized by this incident, nor have I blamed my parents for leaving us with someone they trusted. My message to parents of younger children is that there is no guarantee that their children will be safe from abuse when they are left with supposedly trusted individuals.

Ironically, while living in Kenya, my father and our family again witnessed citizens uprising against the British. In 1952, the Mau Mau revolution shook the British colony. The British spent millions of dollars trying to suppress the rebellion. Several hundred thousand Kenyans were rounded up and sent to concentration camps. Many Kenyans were imprisoned and executed. During the war, British white coffee farmers were also slaughtered during this fight for freedom. On December 12, 1963, Kenya declared its independence from Britain. Jomo Kenyatta, who led the rebellion, became the first Prime Minister of Kenya.[5] To keep us safe during these dangerous times, my father and his friends carried cricket bats for protection and patrolled the neighborhoods, wary of the dangers of the warring political climate. In later years, I was working at a hospital in Valdosta, Georgia. Much to my surprise, one of the nurses, a woman from England, had played soccer with Jomo Kenyatta. What are the chances of meeting someone with such an interesting historical relationship in your workplace?

When I was eleven years old, my father had an opportunity to move to Zambia working for the Ministry of Finance. My mother agreed to move, even though there were very few Indian families living in Zambia at that time. Indian families tend to move near other Indians for support and socialization. After our relocation, my mother found it difficult to find the groceries and spices that were needed to prepare our meals, so she started a vegetable garden. She was able to hire locals for domestic help who lived in another small house on our property.

This family move taught me an important lesson that we should be open to take advantage of opportunities when they present themselves. Sometimes the situation is uncomfortable, but the opportunity must be pursued to get further in life or career. At times, people are reluctant to move away from their comfort zone and then regret not achieving their dreams. Partners should be willing to support each other. My parents were direct opposites. My father was a "can-do" man while my mother was reluctant to try new ventures and take risks. In this situation, she was agreeable to do whatever was necessary for our family's financial stability.

In Zambia, I attended a Catholic convent high school run by German nuns. The Indian teachers in Kenya were much harsher with their corporal punishment. Both were similar in their expectations. Every student knew that he or she would be punished if you did not behave in school. During this time, I had a favorite teacher, Mrs. Arrow. She was an older English woman who took time to give swimming lessons to another student and me before classes started. Swimming is still my favorite form of exercise. Some people play an important role in your life. Even though it may be for a very brief period, they leave a lasting impression. We should cherish these individuals and be thankful for the connection. It is essential to give back to others, to take time to fulfill their needs, especially with those individuals who may be struggling or want to learn. I have cherished what my elders continue to teach me. And in turn, I enjoy imparting some knowledge to those younger than myself, be it cooking, sewing, exercises, medical or career advice.

When I was growing up, I did not get into trouble. Even as a very young student, I maintained a sense of self-discipline. I did not want to disappoint my parents or teachers. I took great pride in my studies. Throughout my career I worked with children. I still struggle to understand students' behaviors like truancy, bullying, making fun of other students, or outright aggression and disrespect towards teachers and parents. Some children are acting out trauma from their home life. Others are trying to fit in with the "cool kids." Within the medical field, there are studies examining if these children were born with dysfunctional wiring of the brain that makes them act out inappropriately. Many of the parents are hard-working individuals and provide for their children, but are dysfunctional in other ways, and do not demonstrate a positive role model for their children. I was very fortunate as a young person; I was not exposed to unruly, aggressive, and self-centered children during my school years.

While in high school, my mother spent a great deal of time teaching us how to cook and sew. I still admire the embroidery she did by hand on napkins and pillowcases. Now most ornate work is done by machines, and it does not hold up or appear as the beautiful hand-crafted work. We had cooking appliances and running hot water now. My mother taught us different Indian customs, traditions, festivals, dances, and other rituals. She focused on educating us about our roles as women. My mother's friend who visited us often, taught us how to enjoy life and have fun. Sadly, she passed away from breast cancer in her forties. I was able to connect with her before she passed away to tell her what a positive influence she had been in my life. Even today, I encourage young people to acknowledge and show appreciation to adults who have offered their knowledge, advice, or monetary assistance. Their generation is more self-centered. They do not understand the value of shared moments until they become just a memory.

During my school years I was exposed to several languages. Education in school was in English. My parents were from the state of Gujrat in India, and we spoke Gujrati at home. Bollywood movies are in Hindi, which is also the official language of India. I learnt to speak, read, and write Hindi and Gujrati in school as well. French and Latin were offered as extra courses and since I enjoyed learning different languages, I also attended these classes. I graduated from high school with four languages and four science subjects, so I would be able to choose a career path in different directions, if necessary. It makes me sad to see so many children who do not speak their parents' or ancestors' language. The parents fear that their children will lag behind in their other school subjects due to the confusion of learning several languages at the same time. This situation could create a lack of communication with grandparents and hinder bonding especially if the elders do not speak English. Being multilingual may help immensely with their children's careers later in life. Older adults are encouraged to learn a new language to open new pathways in the brain, keep them sharp and ward off dementia.

After I finished high school, my parents decided to move to England. Indian children, who were British subjects, were either sent to India or England for further education. The educational degrees bestowed in Zambia would not have been recognized elsewhere in the world, so it was a logical choice to move to England. My mother was already in England with my two older sisters during my final year in high school. My father was in the last year of his contract with the Ministry of Finance in Zambia. When it was time for me to travel from Zambia to England, I stopped off in Kenya to spend a few days with a family friend and his wife.

This visit turned out to be most unfortunate. The family friend was twice my age. His wife was almost eight months pregnant with their first child. I spent my days in the husband's company as he went around town tending to his business. One evening he took me to a drive-in movie and took advantage of me sexually. Instead of flight or fight to this sudden unexpected assault, I froze. I suspect many girls and women freeze during this stressful situation. I did not have the courage or the knowledge to fend him off. The next day I was bleeding, and he took me to a doctor's office and got me a "morning after" pill. The doctor was a friend of his and he never asked me what had transpired. I was in shock; I was not expecting someone in my family whom I trusted to behave this way with me. I could not tell his wife since I did not want to upset her. I also didn't know anyone else in Kenya with whom I could confide in. The man insisted I spend my days with him during the time I was in Kenya before leaving for England. He made the situation worse by bragging to his friends about taking advantage of me and telling me about other girls he had taken advantage of in India. I was very naive in these matters. I never thought that someone I respected and even admired for his outgoing and jovial nature would take advantage of me.

I left Kenya a few days later. I was upset that I let someone abuse me this way He took take away my innocence and left me feeling vulnerable. Like other Indian girls, I had been raised to respect adults and not talk back to them. Elders were always right. We were taught to not speak up, be subservient and tolerate what comes our way. I was responsible for my own destiny and had no one with whom I could share my sad or angry feelings. I decided that I would not let this short unfortunate incident influence my life going forward. However, I would not remain silent in the future and would put a stop immediately to anyone making advances that made me feel uncomfortable. I learnt to be more aware of predators, and I have met several of them in my life since that week in Kenya. Nothing would have been gained or changed if I had informed my family of this most unfortunate event. I remained silent about what I had been subjected to at that time in my life.

There was a brief encounter with the offender at my sister's wedding. I had to resist going over to him and slapping the smirk off his face when he saw me. By this time, I was in medical school and more in control of my actions and emotions.

I did not need to create a scene at a happy occasion. I did not inform my father of this incident until my late forties in an email. At the mention of this man, I had made an angry statement about him to my father. I felt my father was owed an explanation. He was very supportive and there was never again any reference to my perpetrator in our family. My mother and I have never discussed this event, nor do I feel the need to talk to her about it. She would be understanding but at this stage of our lives, nothing would change this unfortunate incident from my youth.

Once I arrived in England, I attended Copeland High School and studied pre-university courses. It was during the very first week at Copeland that I met my future husband, Bipin. He went off to a medical school in Scotland while I secured admission to the Dental School of London. However, Bipin encouraged me to follow him to the University of St. Andrew's medical school. We studied together and worked long hours during summer vacations to save money for the university. I have remained friends with several peers from that time as they were all hard working and responsible individuals. Importance of positive peers cannot be underestimated. Young people are led astray by friends who influence them to drink, do drugs, bully others, disrespect adults and other people's property. Power of peers leading you in a positive direction, to be responsible adults, is invaluable. Bipin and I were the first students selected from our high school to attend medical school. It was a great achievement!

Sadly, around the time when I went to England in 1973, Idi Amin, the President of Uganda, asked all the Indian businessmen and their families to leave Uganda. This decree contributed significantly to the financial demise of the country. Many of the families arrived with only the clothes on their backs and one suitcase. The families were affluent in Uganda but had not been allowed to bring their financial wealth with them. Now they had to start their lives all over again. They were British subjects and were permitted to resettle in England. Many of my new friends at Copeland High school were in this situation. Through hard work and community support, these individuals became successful. In the beginning, they were upset about their predicament. Shortly thereafter, they focused on what they needed to do to achieve their goals in life. I have remained friends with some of these peers over the years. I am happy to see how successful they have become in business and their careers after pursuing advanced education. England has a great educational system. Students are assisted financially with the cost of a university education if their families are unable to afford this expense. However, students need to be motivated to study. In comparison, the cost of undergraduate college in the United States is high. Students can incur a tremendous amount of debt. This major loan expense after graduation from a two or four-year degree program deters many young people from continuing to pursue advanced degrees in graduate school. Although, there are many grants and scholarships available to students with excellent grades.

Medical school brings its own set of challenges. I was also navigating a personal relationship. It was tough for me at times. As a young Indian woman, certain expectations were ingrained into me. They were what I thought to be my responsibilities. I shopped for groceries, cooked, took care of the laundry and other household chores, in addition to my medical studies. Bipin and I did some chores together, but Bipin could focus mainly on his studies and play cricket for the university. Halfway through medical school studies, my parents moved to Florida in the United States. There were no care packages from my family to help me. I became self-reliant and independent without my parents in the U.K. Today I know of several Indian mothers who constantly send packages of prepared meals to their children in college, perpetuating dependence on parents rather than learning to rely on their own ability to cope. To this day, I am guilty of taking on more of the household chores than I should. My 86-year-old mother chooses to spoil me now, making me several food items to bring home after my visits with her. I appreciate all she does, but I have no expectations.

My father chose to leave England at this time because there were no real opportunities for him to start a business. Also, he did not like the weather in England. He had been used to warmer temperatures living near the equator in Kenya and the steady temperatures all year round while living in Zambia. He had always talked about wanting to immigrate to the United States, the land of opportunity. Both my sisters completed their education in England and moved to the United States with my parents to start a new life. My father was able to make the move to the United States due to his profession in accounting. He realized that the only way to make a decent living was to have his own business. My parents settled in Cocoa, Florida and opened a small motel. At that time, many Indian families came to America and opened small "mom and pop" businesses. My father improved the property, and later, sold it at a profit. He then moved to Lakeland, Florida, where he invested in several properties and companies. He helped to settle many relatives in Florida and to establish their own businesses. My parents have lived in Lakeland, Florida for forty plus years, since 1979. Sadly, my father passed away in 2014.

After nine years of dating, Bipin and I married. We were both twenty-five years old, older than most people, who married much earlier in those days. It was a lavish affair with close to four hundred people in attendance. Bipin was an only son, and our culture required a grand celebration. After I completed my medical internship, we decided to immigrate to the United States. In England, it was difficult to establish a private practice as a physician, due to a pyramidal system. In the United States, we could complete our residencies in our specialty, start a private practice, and work for ourselves. Moving to America was a better option for both of us. We had often visited my parents in Florida. I had always intended to move closer to my family. Bipin's parents came to live with us in Augusta, Georgia where we started our residencies. We initially shared some of the housework, but my mother-in-law did most of the cooking. It was helpful that my in-laws were living with us while maintaining a household, but we had little privacy as a married couple. After we completed our residencies, we moved to Valdosta, Georgia to establish our private practices.

Eventually, Bipin and I divorced. After much discussion and sadness, he realized that he should have contributed and assisted me with maintaining our household partnership. Sadly, that was not the only reason for our separation. I had gone through numerous infertility tests to try and conceive a child. I ended up with an ectopic pregnancy. Bleeding from this event caused endometriosis and fibrosis. This medical emergency led to my inability to get pregnant again and left me feeling like a failure. Bipin was an only child, and we had always talked about having a large family. I was a successful physician in my career but felt inadequate in my inability to conceive and have a family. Not having children was not part of our life plan. I used to babysit from a very young age in Zambia and loved babies. This wrench in my personal existence left a gaping hole. Professionally, I was working long hours, starting a private practice, and studying for Medical Board exams. I separated from my husband. I had nothing left to give to the relationship. We lived apart for two years, and then we divorced. At the time, I realized that although we were no longer partners, I still loved him. I have learned through experience that although you may not live with someone anymore, you do not stop loving or caring about this person. After our divorce, I had to make personal adjustments and become fully responsible for myself. During our marriage, Bipin had handled all the financial matters, including our investments. I became adept at managing my affairs. This skill has served me well throughout my lifetime, assisting my father when he became ill and passed away, and now with my mother's financial affairs. Over the years, Bipin and I have remained dear friends which is a great comfort to me. He has known me since I was sixteen years old, a lifetime!

I met my present domestic partner, Stephen, at the hospital where I practiced. We have been together for thirty-one years. We are compatible; we enjoy traveling, sharing similar interests in the foods we enjoy, what shows to watch, exercising and staying fit, and caring for our parents. Most of all, he makes me laugh. We are opposites in many ways as well. I was brought up in a conservative, Indian household while he grew up in the deep South. He is outspoken, and at times, speaks with a brash tone of voice that bothers me. He is independent and hardheaded. However, I sincerely appreciate how caring he is to me and know that we will age gracefully together. Sometimes, he worries too much, which is difficult for me since I pride myself on being self- sufficient. When we are together, we enjoy each other's company, but also give each other space when needed.

In relationships, it is essential to understand what makes your partner happy. There are many couples who are attracted to opposite personalities. This partnership can be very successful since each individual brings different strengths to the relationship. One can provide for the family financially, while the other excels at homemaking and tending to the children's needs. On the other hand, opposites can also become involved in situations leading to 'warfare.' Both parties adopt different priorities. Conflict arises when each person has their own way of doing things. One is organized and the other is disorganized. One is emotional and the partner is stoic. One is a caretaker and the other is needy and wants all the attention. One likes to spend money and the other cannot set limits on the partner's spending habits. One is outgoing and likes to socialize while the partner is reclusive. One has healthy eating habits and exercises while the other is not interested in this lifestyle. Partners with different priorities can create problems for their children. They receive mixed messages from their parents and are confused. They don't know which parent to emulate without causing emotional turmoil with one parent or the other.

I have been retired from my medical practice as a psychiatrist for fourteen years. From the beginning of my practice, I worked long hours and saved for retirement. I was able to retire at the age of fifty-one. I wanted to enjoy life. Too often, doctors continue to work late in life and die shortly after retirement. I did not want to be part of that sad statistic. Ironically, six months after I retired, my father had a severe heart attack. I was devastated and prayed for his recovery and survival. At the time, I realized that I would be responsible for overseeing his business dealings and financial affairs. Fortunately, my father lived another six years. I would drive down regularly from Georgia to take care of my parents in Florida. I was grateful that one of my sisters lived in the same town as my parents and was a tremendous help in day-to-day care of our parents. She still assists in caring for my mother and visits with her every day. My other sister lives in California and is not available. Stephen and I have continued taking care of our parents as they have aged. Role of caring for elderly parents usually falls on the female but there are men like Stephen who are caretakers as well. He travelled from our home to his parent's home regularly for fifteen years tending to their needs. My mother is the only parent who is still alive today.

Eventually, we sold our house in Georgia and moved to the beach in Cape Canaveral, Florida. My father loved visiting us here at the ocean. One of my biggest regrets in life is that he only lived six months after we moved into our home. My partner and I were most fortunate to live for several months with my parents before we moved to Cape Canaveral. During that time, I was able to talk with my father and learn about his life, simplify his financial affairs, and assist my mother. I will always cherish this time together. When my father became very frail, my mother grew stronger emotionally. As I look back on their relationship, they truly complimented each other. My mother never dealt with any paperwork, mail, or writing checks in her life. On the other hand, she teased my father about his inability to make her a cup of tea.

Indian parents are not forthcoming with their emotions. Fortunately, my father had no problems telling us how much he loved us. Both my parents have always been emotionally available, more so after my divorce. They just wanted to see me happy. My mother is now eighty-six years old and chooses to live by herself. It is almost unheard of, for an Indian woman of my mother's age to live by herself, especially when she never learned to drive. With my help and my sister's support, she is happiest in her own home. I stay with her ten days a month. It is a special time for both of us as we spend time talking, cooking, doing yard work, shopping, and watching shows together. American culture has often been described as 'a throwaway society'. It also relates to how many adult children do not take care of their parents in their old age. They place them in nursing homes and rarely visit them. Spending time with our elderly parents and relatives can be such an enriching and rewarding experience filled with cherished memories. We should not waste this valuable time before their passing. Even in medical school, there is an emphasis on curing people. In reference to the aging population, medical students should focus on how to manage their disease, slow its progression, and make them comfortable in order to benefit from additional time with their families.

Looking back on my life and my parents' expectations, my father perceived me as a competent individual, not a male or a female. My mother always refers to me as the son, "she never had." In Indian culture, parents were almost always taken care of by their eldest son. This practice has fallen by the wayside now that the daughters also take care of ailing parents. My father believed that education was paramount to get ahead in life and pushed us to achieve to the best of our abilities. Both my mother and father believed strongly in helping other people to get ahead in life. They had families in need come and live with them or fed them, until they were able to become independent. I have also inherited this quality to assist others with their life journey.

I believe in being tolerant and forgiving to individuals who have hurt me. Remaining angry and unforgiving only hurts yourself. You have to take full responsibility for your mistakes, accept the consequences, and learn from those experiences. You must accept disappointments and not dwell on them. You need to focus on working hard in order to succeed. Do not be complacent with mediocre work. It is important to always show appreciation to those individuals who have assisted you in your personal and professional life. You must take care of yourself, including your physical, mental, and spiritual well-being. You should remember often to reach out to your parents and elders who sacrificed throughout their lifetime to enrich your life. Most parents do their best to meet the needs of their children but obviously some fall short. Sadly, these may turn out to be the children that become society's problems. Most of all, be happy with your family and what you have accomplished in life. Surround yourself with positive people to enjoy and celebrate the various milestones and rewards in your life. Work on being an excellent role model with integrity to influence others. Be strong enough to deal with negative peer pressure and stand up to bullies. Become involved in your community to assist others. Take charge of your own life and destiny!

Now, as I look back, I have lived a happy life. I had many mentors in my life from a young age. My parents, teachers, friends of parents, peers, my ex-husband, old and new friends, and my partner, all have provided me with love and constant support. I continue to challenge myself. Recently, I found the news events around the world and in the United States most disturbing. I decided to write this book about social issues today, including the school shootings and the pandemic that has left so many people dead and injured for life. There is such a division among the citizens in our country. The sexual revolution of the sixties has affected the enormous outpouring of sexual abuse cases in the country. There are issues revolving around people who have and those who do not. Race relations that should have been settled in the 60s, still rage on as documented by the protests and riots following the death of George Floyd in 2020. We are in turmoil about immigration. How did we arrive at this place in 2019 where chaos reigns? The year 2020 brought even more distress with the COVID-19 pandemic, the riots and looting.

"Chaos in the world brings uneasiness, but it also allows the opportunity for growth and creativity."[6]

Tom Barrett

Introduction

Like millions of other people before them, my parents came to the United States of America seeking a better life. America is the land of freedom, opportunity, and democracy. I, too, became a citizen of the United States. I am an American, not an Indian, African, or British citizen based on my family's unique ancestry. Nor do I personally identify myself solely in terms of the female gender; my identity is the sum of my life experiences. However, gender does matter. Men and women experience the world differently. Although gender colors the way we perceive the world around us, we can change that mindset and be open to explore new paradigms.

I find that there is an urgency to write this book now. The "#MeToo Movement" was sweeping the country in 2018. It may be derailing the long-established relationship between men and women. Standing up to an individual who is abusing you physically, sexually, or emotionally is imperative for your total well-being. However, getting carried away with the movement and accusing men of all sorts of abuse and causing the demise of their careers must be addressed. A voice has to be given to those who are too afraid to speak up to the masses. The men and women who are silent, do not necessarily agree with the direction that the movement has taken to uncover every hint of abuse from many years ago. Thousands of women have joined this campaign because it is politically correct. Many of them may fear retribution from the boisterous women leading the charge. In turn, men have stayed deafeningly silent. Individuals must stand up and be the voice of reason. Their concerns must be heard. Additionally, American culture and the relationship between men and women have changed significantly from the middle of the twentieth century after World War II to today in the twenty-first century. Social behaviors in the workplace and within the family that were acceptable then, are no longer tolerable today.

Professionally, I have a deep understanding of this subject matter, not just because of my training as a psychiatrist, but also from my twenty plus years of experience treating numerous patients (children, men, and women). It is essential to understand my background. I was brought up in a very conservative Indian household until the age of sixteen years old. Then I moved with my family to the United Kingdom and eventually, to the United States. By that time, I was fully indoctrinated into western culture. I had exposure to psychiatric patients during medical school rotations in the United Kingdom, four years of psychiatric training in the United States, followed by private practice, which allowed me the opportunity to understand human behaviors in a variety of dysfunctional situations. In my practice, I treated numerous patients who were exposed to a range of abuses. Since I was the only female psychiatrist for fifteen years in my community, abused women sought my help in recovery. At that time, there was no #MeToo Movement. Everyone came with her own set of problems describing how she had been affected, and together, we worked on how she could become healthy again. Some women chose to wallow in their misery and focus on how unfair their life had been. I stayed busy helping patients who wanted to move forward and not let these past abusive incidents control them for the rest of their lives. During an initial evaluation, I would assess the patient's motivation to heal from the trauma she had suffered. Some patients refused to let go of the dysfunction. Refusing to move on allows the patient to use past abuse as a crutch. I set specific goals for each patient. If a patient was unwilling to work toward those goals, I gave the individual the option to come back when she was ready to get help. I would also recommend that additional assistance was available. It takes a very courageous individual to take that first step, ask for help, and to be receptive to therapy for recovery.

I have always preferred the one-on-one approach to address life issues. However, this topic and many other current topics are too important to reach solely one individual at a time. It is essential to reach as many people as I can through the written word. I am fearful, as are others in this country that we are losing the principled values upon which this country was established. Children need to learn discipline. The mass shootings and sexual harassment need to stop. No one should support individuals who abuse others because of their position of power. Both men and women must be empowered to do the right thing and always act appropriately.

Just as the #MeToo Movement has unhinged us as a couple, the anger and racial divide, fueled by politicians who cannot agree on anything and continue to tear at the fabric of American society has unhinged the US. It has made us appear weak, undisciplined, and a laughingstock for others around the globe. Culture refers to the shared attitudes and actions of a particular social group. Social media has created a "Cancel Culture," in the form of group shaming. It refers to the popular practice of withdrawing support for (canceling) public figures and companies after they have done or said something considered objectionable or offensive.[7] People must be held accountable for their actions and behavior, and receive the consequences when they break the rules of society and decency. However, many young people have no knowledge of the history of this country or what their predecessors had to endure to make America the country it is today. They want to rewrite history without even knowing what it is, other than the headlines or few words spread on social media as the gospel truth. When did Facebook and Twitter and other social media outlets become judge and jury, causing many individuals to lose their careers, reputations, or work opportunities after being outed? And with respect to the #MeToo Movement, many people effectively lost their reputations without having the opportunity to clear their name.

Other figures were getting canceled for past racist and anti-LGBTQ remarks.[8]Students were trying to get a professor from the University of Chicago fired because of the remarks he made, but after an investigation by the staff at the University, he was reinstated. Some staff members at Hachette Publishing refused to work on J.K. Rowling's next book after she was smeared as being a "transphobic." She had made a comment about women and her publisher spoke up for her stating "Freedom of speech is the cornerstone of publishing." Social media allows all sorts of freedom of speech, but the cancel culture has gone too far. Critics of canceling feel that people are too quick to judge and ruin lives over mistakes made recently or from many years ago, without knowing all the facts. It has become a way of rejecting anyone you disagree with or someone who did something you did not like. People do not get a second chance. Former President Barack Obama argued that rash social media judgments do not amount to true social activism. The solution is to challenge these people, and those of us who can, must speak up.

Indians believe in destiny and Karma, the spiritual law of cause and effect.[9] This law states that our actions in this life dictate the rewards that we will receive in the next. "You reap what you sow."[10] Good things generally happen to good people. Unfortunately, some people suffer many misfortunes even though they are leading a good life. Indians believe that you pay for the consequences in this lifetime or in the next life for your infractions. This is Karma.

> *"Karma moves in two directions. If we act virtuously, the seed we plant will result in happiness. If we act non-virtuously, suffering results."*[11]
>
> *Sakyong Mipham*

Recently, a friend of mine encouraged me to read Paul Coelho's book *The Alchemist*. I have struggled with various obstacles in my life which I needed to overcome. Writing this book is one of them. "We are told from childhood onward that everything we want to do is impossible!"[12] Now, it is time to put down on paper what concerns me the most in our society today. I questioned whether I had the expertise to be an author. Medically speaking, I am qualified to analyze and treat psychiatric conditions, but was I capable of discussing the social issues of today?

Paulo Coelho writes about: "Fear of realizing the dream."[13] I have spent hours discussing these issues with family and friends. Everyone encouraged me to write what I thought. They felt that what I had to say was necessary to be heard, to be listened to by a broader audience. They realized that I had a passion for these social issues of today. It was time to act. The ideas put forth in this book are my beliefs, in addition to the views of other individuals, results from documented studies and academic articles. I hope my presentation challenges you to look at human behavior from a different perspective. I want to provoke discussions about the issues of sexual ethics, relationships, gun violence, parenting, childrearing, the damage that social media is inflicting, and other societal vows. My hope is that this book will provide you with an understanding of human behavior and tolerance. It expresses different viewpoints about stressful situations in our society. I am asking you to be open-minded and to believe in forgiveness. It is time to contemplate the direction our country is taking. It is up to all of us to make our world a better place.

"Society grows great when old men plant
trees under whose shade they will never sit."[14]
Rabindranath Tagore, Indian Poet

Part 2

Enough is Enough – Get Over It

Sexual Abuse and Molestation

There is no place in any society for any man or woman to be abused, but are we taking the whole concept of abuse "too far?"

"Sexual abuse is an unwanted sexual activity, with perpetrators using force, making threats, or taking advantage of victims not able to give consent. In most instances, victims and perpetrators know each other. Immediate reactions to sexual abuse include shock, fear, or disbelief. Long-term symptoms include anxiety, fear, or post-traumatic stress disorder."[15] When force is immediate, of short duration or infrequent, it is called sexual assault. The offender is referred to as a sexual abuser or molester. "The term covers any behavior by an adult or older adolescent towards a child to stimulate any of the involved sexually. The use of individuals younger than the age of consent for sexual stimulation is referred to as child sexual abuse or statutory rape."[16]

The World Health Organization (WHO), the Center for Disease Control, and the U.S. Department of Justice have conducted studies and reported the prevalence of children being forced to have sex in their lives before the age of eighteen, as 7.9% of males and 19.7% of females.[17] There is a large gender gap of sexual abuse cases between boys and girls. Girls are victimized more often, and boys are reluctant to disclose the abuse. Approximately 30% of the abusers are relatives of the child, most often fathers, stepfathers, uncles, older siblings, or cousins.[18] Around 60% are other acquaintances such as friends of the family, babysitters, or neighbors; 10% are strangers of child abuse victims.[19] Women are reported to commit 14% of sex offense cases against boys and 6% against girls. Child sexual abuse offenders are not pedophiles unless they have a primary or exclusive interest in prepubescent children.[20]

Sexual Harassment

Sexual misconduct can occur when one person uses a position of authority to compel another person to engage in otherwise unwanted sexual activity. Sexual harassment was a term coined in 1975 by a group of women at Cornell University after an employee at the university filed for unemployment benefits after she had resigned. She had accused her supervisor of touching her inappropriately.[21] Nothing happened to her boss, a renowned nuclear physicist. She complained and eventually, through her defense from a women's campus organization and national media attention, the university placed her in another position.

Sexual harassment in the workplace might involve an employee, who is coerced into a sexual situation out of fear of being dismissed. This position is particularly troublesome for a woman who is a single parent, and her family is dependent on her for their financial welfare. It can also involve a student in a school or college, submitting to the sexual advances of a teacher for fear of being punished or receiving a failing grade. In the entertainment industry, an actress can be afraid of not receiving a role in a movie or television program if she does not accept the sexual advances of the movie producer or executive.

In the 1970s, most businesses and institutions had no policies on sexual harassment whatsoever, and even egregious complaints were regularly dismissed. In 1980, the Equal Employment Opportunity Commission (EEOC), the federal agency tasked with enforcing civil rights laws in the workplace, issued guidelines declaring sexual harassment a violation of

Title VII of the Civil Rights Act. "The EEOC continued to focus much of its enforcement efforts on eliminating discriminatory employment systems that operated to exclude racial and ethnic minorities and women. The EEOC was successful in obtaining substantial, widely publicized relief for many victims of discrimination. The affirmative relief required by many of these resolutions helped to motivate appreciable changes to employers' practices."[22] Even with these judicial efforts, it was difficult to lodge a complaint that was resolved.

What separates an illegal act of sexual harassment from merely an annoying interaction between a boss and a subordinate? When does a boss stop being a nuisance and become a criminal? Even now, what constitutes sexual harassment remains murky. Some of the stories clearly cross the line, but others seem more cryptic. When did commenting on the looks of a colleague, or inviting her for a drink, asking about the individual's marriage, touching the arm of a person, or hugging an employee, cross into the boundaries of harassment? Men are now worried about asking questions or making statements in the workplace. "I wonder if I should tell someone that she looks nice, or give a congratulatory hug, or be alone with someone in a room." Now even an innocent comment requires an apology: In 2013, President Barack Obama was recorded referring to Harris as the "best-looking attorney general in the country." He later apologized after critics labeled the comment as sexist.

This national focus on sexual harassment has changed the workplace atmosphere. Individuals' behavior among staff members is now guarded and circumspect. Everyone is aware of the consequences of inappropriate behavior and sexual advances. In just a minute, one's career can be destroyed. Ironically, the action may have been an innocent gesture, interpreted as a sexual advance to the employee. Without witnesses, it is one person's version of the story against the other's interpretation. While everyone wants to flush out the serial predators and rapists, there is a risk of being suspicious of all interactions. What happens when someone who makes a sexist joke is regarded as just as guilty of sexual harassment in comparison to the boss who fondles an employee? Neither behavior should be encouraged, nor should they be considered as equal.

At the end of 2018, the EEOC reported a 14% increase in harassment cases from 2017, for a total of 7,500 cases.[23] As of January 1, 2020, in the state of California, regulated by law, employers must provide sexual harassment prevention instruction to all employees once every two years. They must also provide education to seasonal employees, temporary workers, and employees who are hired to work for less than six months. Employers can design the courses or direct their employees to the online courses sponsored by the California Department of Fair Employment and Housing. The classes are available in English and other languages. Also, the employees will receive a certificate upon completion of the training to submit to their employers.[24]

The #MeToo Movement began in 2006; Tarana Burke came up with the phrase to promote the recognition of women who had survived sexual violence. Ten years later, the movement picked up momentum, incited and destroyed the reputations of powerful men and a few women in politics and the entertainment industry.[25] In October 2019 alone, Representative Katie Hill from California chose to resign due to inappropriate sexual relations with a subordinate. Cuba Gooding, the actor, faces a new undisclosed charge in a sexual misconduct case. A new book will be released detailing information about Matt Lauer's firing and providing the details surrounding the rape of Brooke Nevils, the NBC News employee by Lauer.[26] There are a fair number of sexual abuse cases stemming from the victims' childhoods, including many prominent actresses.

Childhood Abuse and Abuse
Continuing into Adulthood

Any intentional mistreatment of a child under 18 years old is considered child abuse. Many forms of child abuse exist. A child experiences physical abuse when the child is purposely, physically injured, or placed at risk by another individual. Sexual abuse with a child includes fondling, oral-genital contact, intercourse, exploitation, or exposure to pornography. Continuing to berate a child with verbal and emotional assault, in addition to isolating, ignoring, or rejecting a child, are all forms of emotional abuse. Medical abuse occurs when someone provides false information about a child's health and insists on medical attention for the child, placing the child in danger of unnecessary medical procedures. This is diagnosed as Munchausen Syndrome by proxy. Child neglect includes the failure to provide food, clothing, shelter, affection, supervision, medical, or dental care for the child.[27]

When children are abused at a young age, they are too young to understand what is happening to them. They become fearful, have nightmares, suffer from anxiety, develop behavioral issues in school, display oppositional behaviors, and experience bedwetting, in addition to other negative conduct. These children do not speak up since there is a "secret bond" between the perpetrators and themselves. They are most likely being abused by someone they are familiar with or know very well. The offenders have most probably threatened to harm the children or their parents, or even tell the children's parents that the child has been doing something "wrong." The children become frightened that they will get into trouble. Children may continue with the abuse since it constitutes a "special relationship," and they are receiving a fair amount of exclusive attention. What child does not want to feel special, despite the general discomfort and anxiety accompanying this relationship? It is difficult for any child to talk about the abuse or report it to anyone.

What happens to these children who were abused? Some of them grow up and realize that what had transpired was wrong. They understand that they were not to be blamed for the abuse and that the adult in the relationship should have known better. They live with the "bad memory," but do not let it control and consume them for the rest of their life. They go on to be successful adults, hopefully not letting anyone else abuse or take advantage of them ever again. Often, they never tell anyone about the abuse, but bury it in the far recesses of their memory. Most of the children who were abused in this category, experienced the trauma in a very benign, non- threatening way. In these cases, the harm consists mainly of inappropriate touching, rarely any sexual penetration. Generally, the adult who was abusing them was kind, loving, and even gave them rewards and treats. The children are left with very perplexed feelings for the perpetrator.

> *"Forgive others not because they deserve forgiveness, but because you deserve peace."*[28]
>
> *Jonathan Lockwood Huie*

The second type of individual who was abused as a child is affected in some way from the abuse. The child was "awakened sexually" from a young age, when the abuse started. In these cases, there is a good chance that penetration took place. The perpetrator was again someone familiar with the child or teenager. Not understanding how to control these sexual urges, they set out trying to seduce other adults or begin exploring sexual activity with other children their age. Sometimes young children "play" and are acting out what was done to them. Some of these children grow up to be very promiscuous adults, having multiple sex partners. They are trying to negate the trauma while others are trying to relive the sexual experience that was extremely exciting to them. After all, the body is going to react, giving pleasurable sensations, even if the act was not one, they anticipated or initiated.

> *"I forgive people, but that does not mean I accept their behavior or trust them. I forgive them for me, so I can let go and move on with my life."*[29]
>
> *Author Unknown*

In many cases of abuse of females by fathers, stepfathers or family friends, the daughters tend to get alienated from their mothers. This is due to the anger stemming from their belief that the mothers did not protect them from the abuse. They also assume that the mother will not believe them. The abused females may never discuss the issue of being abused with the mother. The women go through life holding onto that anger and resentment, unable to have a relationship with the mother. Both miss out on the special bond that exists between a mother and daughter.

This does not have to be the case if trust exists, and the issues are addressed. Depending on the family dynamics and the situation the mother finds herself facing, she may not be able to do anything. That will also create conflict that may last a lifetime.

> *"Do not judge people for the choices they make when you do not know the options they had to choose from".*[30]
>
> *Author Unknown*

Sexual abuse of male children is under-reported. Males are taught to deal with hardships differently than females. They are more ashamed that they were not strong enough or emotionally able to stop the abuse if the violation was with another male. The situation is a little different when an older female seduces a younger male, even if he is under the legal age limit. Most young boys fantasize about this type of encounter, and they are certainly not going to feel like they were abused, even if their parents feel differently about this encounter. When we hear news about female teachers having sex with young male students, they often claim that they are in love with their teacher. Some adult males have fond memories of the sexual experiences that they had with these teachers, mainly if the abuse occurred in a very loving way and taught them how to become sexually active. Otherwise, young males learn about sex from pornographic magazines, videos, cable television, or even shows like the "Game of Thrones," where nothing is left to the imagination.

> *"Never regret anything that has happened in your life. It cannot be changed, undone, or forgotten. So, take it as a lesson and move on. What's done is done! What's gone is gone! One of life's lessons is always to move on. It is okay to look back and remember but keep moving forward."*[31]

> *Author Unknown*

Recovery from Childhood Abuse

Individuals experience the most distress when an abusive incident that took place, even for a short time, controls their feelings for the rest of their lives. You may not be able to control someone's negative behavior, but you can control how long you participate in it. Emotionally charged memories stay with us a lot longer than ones that do not evoke emotions. It is easy to tap into emotions and memories when thinking of incidents that make you angry, sad, or happy. Memories are easy to retrieve when recalling how someone hurt your feelings or did something unexpected to bring you great joy. People have great difficulty getting past emotions laden with the pain and hurt from abuse. The challenge is not to let any single event in your life control or taint everything else in your life.

In psychiatric practice, patients who were abused, sexually assaulted in an aggressive manner, or penetrated by adults whom they trusted like fathers, stepfathers, uncles, or older brothers struggle a great deal to recover. They cannot reconcile how they could have been treated in such a deplorable manner. An unknown author said: "The worst feeling in the world is knowing you were abused and lied to by someone whom you trusted." A response to that comment is: "No, the worst feeling is allowing it to happen the second time."

"In order to escape accountability for his crimes, the perpetrator does everything in his power to promote forgetting. If secrecy fails, the perpetrator attacks the credibility of his victim. If he cannot silence her absolutely, he tries to make sure no one listens."[32]

Judith Lewis Herman

If the victim is in a position of dependence on the perpetrator for her/his welfare, housing food, schooling, etc., then the abuse may continue for an extended period over which they have little control. Sometimes women will grow up, leave home, get married, do well emotionally, but then fall apart when their daughter comes of age, the time when they were abused. The whole defense mechanism that has helped them survive until now falls apart, and they break down emotionally. They obsess about the abuse and have great difficulty getting past the associated feelings of shame, being used, and feeling dirty.

The intense feelings of shame arise from the pleasurable sensations that are automatically generated by the body. The body is going to respond whether you want it to or not. If you are repeatedly exposed to the sexual situation, the body is going to go into a self-preservation mode. Many women are going to disagree with this analysis, but it is one of the most challenging things to come to terms with understanding sexual abuse. Maybe it is like kidnapping situations when the victims start relating to and sympathizing with the kidnappers.

The most difficult patients to treat are the ones who are sometimes diagnosed with "conversion disorder." It is a mental condition in which a person has blindness, paralysis, or other nervous symptoms that cannot be explained by medical evaluation.[33] Sigmund Freud described this condition as "hysteria" in 1895 when he developed the concept of conversion of psychological problems into somatic manifestations with a strong sexualization of hysteria.[34] Initially, he believed that actual abuses had taken place, but later launched a 'fantasy' theory to explain the development of hysterical symptoms without the necessity of actual abuses. It was Freud who proposed that the memory of trauma which the patient fails to confront because it will cause too much anguish, can be converted into physical symptoms. What is most surprising is that cases like that are typical of those routinely seen by neurologists today.[35] Since we can use sophisticated medical testing today, we now know that it is not the neurological "hardware" that is damaged, so it must be the "software," the psychological response to the meaning of trauma that leads to conversion disorder.

In 2016, researchers discovered that patients with conversion disorder had experienced a greater number of stressful events than other people, and a dramatic increase in these events near to the time when their symptoms began.[36] After ten years of practice, Freud came to believe that behind every hysterical symptom, such as convulsions, paralysis, blindness, epilepsy, amnesia, pain, or aphasia, lay a hidden trauma or series of traumas. Freud's compassion lives on to this day in the method that he established for bringing the disturbing memories to light and reducing their negative and sometimes debilitating effects: psychoanalysis.[37]

Sexual Abuse and Celebrities

What has been very disturbing in the news and the media is the number of celebrities coming forward and reporting sexual abuse. Molly Ringwald put it aptly that at the age of fourteen years old, "at a time when I was trying to figure out what it meant to be a sexually, viable young woman, at every turn some older guy tried to help speed up the process."[38]

In December 2017, TIME Magazine awarded the "Person of the Year" to the "Silence Breakers," the numerous women and men who came forward to relate their experiences with sexual harassment and abuse.[39] Ashley Judd had been speaking out about Harvey Weinstein's attempt to coerce her into bed in 1997 just before her career took off. She told everyone but recalls a screenwriter telling her that Weinstein's behavior was an open secret passed around for years on a whisper network in Hollywood. Finally, in October 2017, Judd went on record about Weinstein's behavior in the New York Times and became the first star to do so. The world listened.[40]

It is incredible that these confident women, whom you would consider self-assured, felt they had no recourse.[41] The situation would appear to be unbearable for a cleaning woman to speak out after being harassed by a co-worker or boss. She must remain silent for fear of losing her job, maybe the only one she has and needs it to support her children. What about an administrative assistant who repeatedly has to fend off her boss, who won't take "no" for an answer, and the hotel housekeeper who has to constantly worry about being accosted by a guest as she goes about her work replacing towels and cleaning bathrooms? Even though this issue has been ever present in society for years, it has finally surfaced to the forefront. Enough is enough. Women have had it with the fear of retaliation and being fired because they refused to cooperate with their abuser. Over the years, thousands of women have been fired and lost their incomes. They have decided to put an end to this practice of abuse. These women have not only described the vulgarity of the harassment and exploitation, but the years of lewd comments, forced kisses, opportunistic gropes, and psychological problems experienced from those advances. Most of the women who were interviewed for the article, "The Silence Breakers," described struggling with a sense of shame. They all wondered: Had they asked for it? Could they have averted the sexual advance? Were they making a big deal out of nothing? They continued to wonder: What just happened? Why didn't they react?[42]

Most actresses choose to look sexy in the way they dress and blame men for looking at them, making comments, and touching them inappropriately. However, the message that they are sending is "look at me!" If men have been allowed to touch women inappropriately without any consequences or established limits, they will repeat this behavior. It is up to the females to put a stop to this behavior regardless of the results. If women ignore their gut instincts, they will get into trouble. Women cannot allow men to touch them and make them feel uncomfortable. They cannot merely excuse this behavior and refuse to report the incident because they want something, like an acting role or a job promotion.

Over the last decade, sexual scenes are almost a must for most movies, and now nudity, both male and female are portrayed on cable television as well. It is difficult to feel sorry for actresses and actors who are getting paid vast sums of money "to bare it all to the world to see and display very intimate acts of sex." At the same time, they are filmed by a camera crew who are watching them on the set. How can one expect men and even women not to make crude comments, feel horny, get erections, or have lustful thoughts?

Women report that they are shamed, called uptight, nasty, bitter, unable to take a joke, are too sensitive when males make crude comments. However, women who want equality and to share the same work environment with men will need to become more thick-skinned and learn to set appropriate limits. Just complaining and acting like victims at the slightest infraction is not going to give women the backbone that they will need. Having the tenacity to stop the abuse before it starts and taking the consequences to standing up for yourself will move them forward in the long run.

> *"It is easy to judge the mistakes of others.*
> *Difficult to recognize our own mistakes."*[43]
> *Author Unknown*

Jennifer Lawrence reported a "degrading and humiliating" experience with producers and casting directors early on in her career. She was instructed to lose fifteen pounds in two weeks for a part in a movie. "During this time, a FEMALE producer had me do a nude line up with about five other women who were much thinner than me. We stood side-by-side with only pasties covering our privates."[44] When she complained to another producer about this incident, he remarked that she was "perfectly f*ckable!"[45] Obviously, it was not the support she wanted to hear. At the time, she reasoned that she let herself be treated a certain way for her career. Men are also asked to change their appearance for a role. Men tend to tolerate rough language more comfortably and joke about crude comments, so producers do not have to be sensitive around them.

In Jennifer Lawrence's previously mentioned case, is it an abuse of authority? The producers wanted a particular look in an actress for the role. They were comparing females. Jennifer asked for an opinion; she received a response. It was not what she wanted to hear. Does that make it abuse? Ask yourself why so many actresses are speaking up when they work in a sex and violence-driven entertainment industry, where anything goes. Do they expect men to see this nudity and not respond as men do? Biologically, men are much more visually stimulated sexually than women. They are expected to keep their mouths shut and stop getting a "hard-on" when explicit sex scenes are shot in the movie and television studios. Actresses must remember that they are paid large sums of money for their performances. If they do not like the work environment that they have perpetuated, these individuals should work in another field, or learn how to set limits, and realize that they may not receive certain acting parts. The actresses must decide how far they are willing to go and stop complaining when they want to work in a sexually charged industry.

Erica Tempesta of the Daily Mail on April 13, 2018, reported another inflammatory comment by Karl Lagerfeld, an

84-year-old German Chanel designer. He was defending a stylist Karl Templer, who was accused of sexual misconduct. A model had claimed that Templer "aggressively pulled down their underwear without asking them" in an exposé published by the Boston Globe in February.[46] Lagerfeld revealed in a candid interview with "Numero" magazine that he was fed up with the #MeTooMovement." He was quoted as saying: "I read somewhere that now you must ask a model if she is comfortable with posing. It is simply too much; from now on, as a designer, you cannot do anything. It is unbelievable. If you do not want your pants pulled about, do not become a model! Join a nunnery, and there will always be a place for you in the convent. They're even recruiting!"[47]

Could he have made his point in a better way? Certainly! Other designers in the industry were upset by his comments. He stated further: "When you are running a billion-dollar business, you must keep up. And if it doesn't suit you, then you may as well be messing around in your bedroom."[48] Models choose a lifestyle of glamor, wear very scant outfits, expose a good part of their bodies to the world but then want the male coworkers to be "gentle" with them in the high- powered, high-tension workplace. Some individuals were suggesting boycotting Chanel. With Chanel's long-standing reputation, that is not going to happen.

Monica Lewinsky published an article in Vanity Fair entitled "Monica Lewinsky: Emerging from the 'House of Gaslight' in the Age of #MeToo" in March 2018. It was almost twenty years after her relationship with President Bill Clinton, the most powerful man on the planet at the time. They had a consensual sexual relationship. She was twenty-two years old. It was her first job out of college. He was her boss and twenty-seven years her senior. She later understood that there were power differentials between the two of them. He was the president, and she was a White House intern. Looking back, she feels she had a limited understanding of the consequences of "maintaining a long-term extramarital relationship" with the President. In 2014, Monica wrote an essay in the same magazine, in which she wrote: "Sure, my boss took advantage of me, but I will always remain firm on this point; it was a consensual relationship. Any 'abuse' came in the aftermath when I was made a scapegoat to protect his dominant position."[49]

In light of the #MeToo Movement, she now sees how problematic it was that the two of them even got to the place where there was a question of consent. She states that in 1998, women were living in times when women's sexuality was a marker of owning their desire. She feels that if she saw herself as a victim in any way, it would open the choruses of "see, you did service him." It is interesting to note that Lewinsky admits to consensual sex. Most young women would get excited at the prospect of a good-looking powerful man being sexually interested in them. Now with the #MeToo Movement, she is questioning her desires and infatuation with "the most powerful man on the planet." She should have stuck to her ownership of desire instead of becoming one of the women saying, "#MeToo!" There is some truth in women needing to be viewed as victims, rather than just being human and enjoying the intimacy of a sexual encounter.

Is it logical for society to feel sorry for people who put themselves on the screen in compromising and sexually explicit poses, and then complain that someone made a comment, touched them inappropriately, or propositioned them? The film industry is an escape into fantasy. It does not represent what real people must deal with on a day-to-day basis.

Women need to be empowered so they can become educated, trained in professions, and rise in the ranks of the corporate world. They must be able to fend for themselves and not be dependent on men or a punching bag for their mates. Women should be given the right to drive. They should not have their genitalia mutilated as is the custom in some African tribes, so they cannot enjoy sex, and the men can control them.[50] There still exists in the 21st century a sex slave-trade industry. There is an organization, "Operation Underground Railroad," whose mission is to lead the fight to end modern-day slavery.[51] In Turkey, women are fighting the politicians to stop being treated as domestic slaves and the freedom for men to beat women at will. In 2020, 205 women in Turkey have been killed. In 2019, 417 died in domestic violence cases, according to activist reports.[52] These are heart-wrenching issues that need much more exposure than comments from women like "he made me feel uncomfortable, invaded my private space, touched my shoulder, smelt my hair." Do not put yourself in that situation! Keep your distance. Let us get our priorities straight.

Sexual Abuse and Children

The state of Florida and public institutions such as the Miami-Dade School district have joined forces and partnered with Lauren's Kids, a south Florida-based-non-profit to develop and produce "It's OK to Tell" campaign. This information provides an effective way to reach parents who do not know or who do not think that they need to address child sexual abuse with their children. "The program is designed to empower children to identify and avoid traps set by child predators, and to speak up and get help if they are hurt."[53]

1. Signs of abuse include frequent bruises, school absences, inadequate personal hygiene, fear of certain people, places, and regressive behavior.
2. It is everyone's legal responsibility to report suspected abuse. Call 1-800-799-7233 (National Domestic Violence Hotline) or the local abuse hotline to report any incidents.
3. "Stranger danger" is obsolete! In more than 90% of abuse cases, children are suffering injury at the hands of someone they know and trust. Teach your children to look for situations or behaviors that make them feel unsafe, and to always tell a grown-up, buddy, parent, or caretaker in these instances.
4. Talk to your child about safe vs. unsafe secrets. Safe secrets will be told eventually.
5. Dangerous secrets will never be told and make you feel icky and confused.

6. Develop a "trusted triangle" with your child, a list of three or more trusted adults in your child's life that he or she can go to about anything they are feeling.

The abuse statistics for children are extremely high. One in three girls and one in five boys are sexually abused before the age of eighteen. The data is staggering, but the solution is clear. With education and awareness, we can prevent 95% of sexual abuse. If children are taught at an early age to speak up and be confident, we may not have so many women having to deal with sexual harassment in their adulthood.

Sexual Abuse and Personal Responsibility

The main thing to remember is that you have a responsibility as an adult to protect yourself. If you have continued accepting abuse from an individual, you must ask yourself what benefits you are gaining from this abuse. Are you looking to get your five minutes of fame by joining the #MeToo Movement? That is not the answer. Not every comment or touch should be construed as abuse. Sometimes, it is just a comment. Although it may be something you do not approve of, it does not rise to the level of harassment or abuse. Crying foul or making a big deal of it is not helping the credibility of the #MeToo Movement. The illogical conclusions drawn from some statements like the following give rise to tensions in the workplace: "By complementing a woman on her appearance in a professional setting, you are reinforcing sexist beliefs about women's worth - that first and foremost, women must be attractive, and this is a primary function of their social role." Another one is "When an older male colleague tells a junior female colleague 'You look so young' or 'You look like a student,' the comment focuses attention on her appearance rather than on her credentials, and it may subtly undermine her authority on the job."[54] When you give yourself these false messages, you are reading more into the comments than is warranted.

You must ask yourself why it is necessary for you to bring up issues from many years ago. Do you want justice now or are you looking for a group for sympathy? Ask yourself what problems you need to get past. By joining this movement, will it help you to live a more peaceful life? The most important question: Have you forgiven yourself?

Lots of bad things happen to many people. There are two types of pain: one that hurts you and the other that changes you. The challenge for every abused individual is to decide which pain they will choose to hold onto. Journaling is an excellent way to get rid of unwanted intrusive thoughts that interfere with your functioning. By writing down these thoughts every day, eventually, you will get sick of writing the same thing repeatedly. Try to allocate time every day to focus on these negative and hurtful thoughts. Repetitive thoughts are like a tape playing in your head, again and again, all day. To get rid of this "tape," you must get it out of your head, onto paper, and do it daily until you no longer need to do it.

Dr. Candace Norcott, PhD said, "People can recover from childhood sexual abuse, but there is no single path or timeline to recovery for everyone. Forming a relationship with a therapist or counselor can be healing at a time when it feels like getting close to someone has been unsafe in the past."[55]

The Catholic Church and
Sexual Abuse of Children

Growing up in Lusaka, Zambia, my older sisters and I attended a Catholic high school run by German nuns. The nuns were extremely strict and did not tolerate any misbehavior. Punishment was doled out with rulers. Sometimes you had to stand on a chair at the back of the classroom. If you were in a lot of trouble, you were sent out of the classroom to the principal's office. Most of us behaved; we did not want to suffer any humiliation. Our uniform was a pinafore dress, worn just above our knees. However, even today, girls attending some Catholic schools must wear short skirts as part of their uniform. Some skirts have to be two and a half to three inches above the knee. Why is this dress code necessary, with the length of the skirt being so short?

At our school we were taught to be ladies and held accountable for our actions. Reports from other people, who attended Catholic mixed schools said that the staff at the schools took significant measures to ensure the well-being and safety of every child. There was never an opportunity to get into trouble. No child was ever left alone with another adult, which avoided any sexual abuse situations. Attending school was an enjoyable experience. These students received a much better education than other students in their community who did not go to a Catholic high school. Our school was a private school for girls only. We did receive the best education available at the time. We were most fortunate and did not suffer from any childhood sexual abuse by the nuns. However, this was not the case for thousands of Catholic school children around the United States and the world.

A Pennsylvania grand jury released a report in August 2018 detailing decades of alleged sexual abuses by priests and cover-ups by diocesan bishops.[56] The bishops and individuals in authority did everything they could to convince the sexual abuse victims not to report the abuse incidents and for law enforcement not to investigate the abuse charges. The abuse included three hundred priests violating children over the course of seventy years.[57] After this report came out, Pope Francis issued a letter six days after acknowledging "with shame and repentance" the Catholic Church's failure to act, putting out a statement stating: "we showed no care for the little ones; we abandoned them."[58] Looking ahead, the pontiff said the Church was working on a "zero tolerance" on abuse and cover-ups. He added: "If in the past, the response was one of omission, today we want solidarity, in the deepest and most challenging sense, to become our way of forging present and future history."[59]

In May 2018, Pope Francis called all the bishops from Chile to come to the Vatican in Rome after he received a 2,300-page report detailing sexual abuse by priests throughout the country. In a three-day emergency summit at the Vatican, they discussed these allegations of abuse. All thirty-four of Chile's active and retired bishops offered their resignations to the Pope.[60] Similar stories of abuse by priests were reported in Australia, Dominican Republic, The Netherlands, Austria, Germany, Spain, Switzerland, and Brazil, home of the world's largest Catholic population.[61]

An article in the Daily Beast, in December 2019 discussed the secret sex lives and sexual abuse of nuns. Pope Francis admitted earlier in 2019 for the first time that the sexual abuse of nuns by priests and bishops was a far bigger problem than the Church had previously conceded. Some sisters were even kept as sex slaves, suffering years of unthinkable abuse and terror.[62] In February 2019, the Vatican magazine, "Women Church World," published an exposé that uncovered hundreds of stories of nuns forced to have abortions, and in some cases, raising their children secretly in the nunneries while pretending that the children were orphans.[63]

The reputation of Catholic priests is rampant with sexual abuse. One wonders if this issue will receive more attention in the wake of the #MeToo Movement. The Catholic Church and the Pope have admitted the problems of abuse. These issues have not been totally resolved in the minds of the Catholic parishioners around the world. Priests and bishops have resigned. Victims have received millions of dollars to settle their cases. More than twenty Catholic dioceses and religious orders have turned to Chapter 11 bankruptcy to negotiate payments to more than 4000 victims who have come forward in the United States.[64]

The Pope has asked for forgiveness for what he called "abuses of power, conscience, and sexual abuse perpetrated by members with roles of responsibility in the church," during the first papal visit in 2018 to Ireland in thirty-nine years.[65] He came face-to-face with the national anger and grief expressed by the Irish people caused by decades of abuse. Often the Pope's reply is simply silence and prayer. Are people more forgiving because these priests and bishops are "people of God?" If anything, these individuals should be held to an even higher standard of decency. I do not see as much anger and publicity generated as the #MeToo Movement. The Catholic Church must make amends in other ways for hiding and perpetuating this abhorrent behavior around the world. Victims should be demanding significant settlements. The Catholic Church is the largest Christian organization with a net worth of $30 billion estimated in 2019.[66] The Church should be sponsoring workshops for parents around the globe to educate parents about symptoms children may demonstrate if they have been abused. The victims should receive free psychological counseling for as long as it is necessary for their recovery. The Church should be offering scholarships and free college tuition to the children who suffered from the abuse. And if they are now adults, provide the tuition or skills training to their children. The Catholic Church needs to implement programs immediately to ensure and protect the children from sexual predators.

University Athletes and Sexual Abuse

After numerous reports of high-profile abuse cases of college athletes, both men and women, maybe it should now be mandated that sports physicians have another staff member present in the examining room when treating or examining athletes. During routine physical examinations, whether they are gynecological or physical, what does an athlete do if he or she feels that they have been touched inappropriately, or the physician has lingered too long on one part of the body? It was reported in May 2018, that the University of Southern California is now facing over half a dozen sexual abuse lawsuits from women athletes who reported being victimized by the assigned physician gynecologist.[67] We will continue to hear about an onslaught of sexual abuse cases against college physicians, even after they are dead and cannot defend themselves!

Dr. Robert Anderson was University of Michigan's wrestling, football, hockey, and track teams' doctor. He worked at UM from 1968 to 2003, before dying in 2008. During the time he worked at the school, he allegedly abused hundreds of students, most of whom were young men, according to attorney Parker Stinar. Former athletes claimed Dr. Anderson would examine their genitalia for unrelated problems and injuries. Many students did not speak up because they were angry, embarrassed, and ashamed. Now a lawsuit has been filed against the university and its Board of Regents. Former athletes will enter mediation with the university this fall, Stinar said. The university knew of the abuse but did not intervene. How do they prove that the young men are telling the truth or is this another shake down, making money for the lawyer and students?[68]

Dr. Larry Nasser, a former Michigan State University physician, a convicted serial child molester, was charged with twenty-two counts of first-degree criminal sexual misconduct. Over 150 women and even a young man from the gymnastic world came forward during his trial and accused him of sexual abuse. He was sentenced to up to 175 years for decades of abuse.[69] Many of the women did try to report their concerns to the organizations that were sponsoring them, like the USA Gymnastics, the US Olympic Committee and Michigan State University. Their complaints were ignored and brushed aside.[70]

While Dr. Nasser's victims continued to come forward to report his alleged abuse, there was an interview on television between a female news individual and an orthopedic doctor. The female journalist was trying to ask the doctor to comment on Dr. Nasser's massage techniques and joint manipulations. She was trying her best to force the doctor to say that it was inappropriate for Dr. Nasser to have his hands on the patient's buttocks, inner thighs and other personal areas of the body when manipulating the hip joints. The orthopedic doctor reported that these were appropriate methods to be used for joint manipulation, and he could not comment about any reported abuse by Dr. Nasser. Media does tend to inflame stories. The more shocking news about a case provides increased viewership, which also brings added revenues through advertising.

Dr. Nasser was a Doctor of Osteopathic Medicine and performed osteopathic manipulation, in which a doctor uses his or her hands to move a patient's muscles or joints with techniques that include stretching, gentle pressure, and resistance. He was accused and convicted of sexual misconduct, whereby he engaged in sexual penetration with many of his victims under the age of sixteen. He acted in a position of authority over the victim, in addition to coercing the victim to submit to his activities.[71] Without a doubt, Dr. Nasser performed numerous cases of sexual abuse against young women. However, there is a fine line to decipher as to who was abused or who just felt uncomfortable when their bodies were touched, joints were manipulated, or sore muscles were massaged. How many of the 150 women were really abused or caught up in the hysteria of the accusations? Many of the parents of these young girls were often present in the room when Dr. Nasser was treating their children.

In May 2018, the sexual abuse victims of Dr. Nassar and the lawyers received $500 million from Michigan State University as a settlement. It is believed to be the most massive sum ever reached in a sexual abuse case involving an American university. It was by far more substantial than the settlements of the sexual abuse cases at Penn State University and from the Catholic Church in the US. The abuse by Dr. Nasser was more than just manipulation and touching. John Manly, the lawyer, for many of the 332 women in Dr. Nasser's case concluded: "I think the number being so large sends a message that it is undeniable, that something terrible happened here, and that Michigan State owns it. When you pay half a billion dollars, it is an admission of responsibility."[72]

Women who were abused by Nasser still have other lawsuits pending against USA Gymnastics, the United States

Olympic Committee, and other organizations and individuals. With the amount of money at stake, there will undoubtedly be other accusers. Anyone who had been involved with these organizations will come forward to demand their share of the financial windfall.

Olympic Gymnasts and Abuse

USA Gymnastics became the most dominant women's program for decades under the tutelage of Béla and Márta Károlyi, who had defected from Romania. The Károlyi Ranch, once known as the breeding ground for Olympic champions, was officially closed as the US Women's Team National Training Center as of January 2018 after the sexual abuse revelations and conviction of Dr. Larry Nasser, the former USA Gymnastics Team doctor.[73] Also, the Károlyi's coaching methods were criticized, and a lawsuit also accused them of turning a blind eye to the molestations of Dr. Nasser.[74] Athletes stated that they created a toxic environment on the ranch where the abuse was able to thrive. The ranch, North of Houston, served as the training site since 2001, was officially certified as the Olympic training site in 2011. The Károlyi's athletic center played a crucial role in the building of the American women into an international powerhouse team in the field of gymnastics that rivaled the teams of Russia, Romania, and China. Béla and Márta Károlyi said that they were not at fault. Béla had retired from coaching in the 1990s and as Team USA's national coordinator in 2001. Márta retired after the Olympic Games in Rio in 2016. They were responsible for coaching many of the USA's biggest gymnastic stars and molding them into Olympic champions. The US women have won 79 World and Olympic medals from 2001 to 2012 under the coaching staff of the Károlyis. The culture and reputation of American women's gymnastics changed drastically. Dvora Myers in her book, "The End of the Perfect 10," points out that before the Károlyis took over the gymnastics program in the United States, Americans performed just satisfactorily in the sport. The gymnasts were not disciplined, physically fit, or accomplished athletes with a strong work ethic. At the Olympics in 1984, Béla Károlyi was the individual coach of the overall champion, Mary Lou Retton, and uneven bars gold medalist Julianne McNamara. Béla and Márta had a reputation for being harsh. Some gymnasts have stated that they were firm but fair. They were outspoken and very selective about whom they trained. They did not select underage gymnasts.[75]

This professional couple dedicated their lives to the sport of gymnastics in Romania and the United States. As of December 2018, the governing body of USA Gymnastics filed for bankruptcy, facing mounting legal and financial challenges.[76] More than 300 women and girls have sued USA Gymnastics, alleging that the organization failed to protect them from Dr. Larry Nasser's abuse. Filing for Chapter 11 protection offered the organization an opportunity to equitably resolve the claims and allocate the insurance proceeds among the claimants in an orderly manner. "The bankruptcy filing will suspend all lawsuits by Nasser survivors and their ongoing efforts to discover the truth about whom at USA Gymnastics and the US Olympic Committee knew about Nasser's criminal conduct and failed to stop it."[77]

Many other professionals work in the field of medicine and touch the human body as part of their treatments. Will massage therapists and physical therapists be required to have other medical personnel in the treatment rooms for fear of similar accusations of abuse in the future? There are no marks left after a massage or therapy. The violation cannot be clearly proved. False accusations can tarnish and destroy one's professional reputation forever. Individuals can also lose their state licenses. Sometimes, for very unhealthy reasons, patients have ulterior motives to instigate an abuse case. With the extreme number of abuse cases being publicized, one wonders what the future will be for medical treatment. Will males and females be segregated and treated solely by a medical staff of the same gender?

> *"Change comes from constructive thought and sound action; not just by complaining or thinking that someone else should do something else."*[78]
>
> *Author Unknown*

Identity and Gender Autonomy

Both sides of the #MeToo Movement need to be heard. Kris Gage explained in a recent article, "How the Women's Conversation Isn't Helping," because one set of demands, conventional femininity, is being replaced by another set, women's empowerment. These feminist movements are not every woman's fight, nor does every woman feel comfortable adopting and embracing their calls to unite. Gage calls herself a feminist, but clearly states she does not want to be labeled. She prefers "identity autonomy," the freedom to be human. Although thousands of women have joined these all-important women's conversations and movements, it does not mean that if she chooses not to join in, that she is sleeping with the enemy. Gender role fluidity is confusing and uncomfortable for many people. Today, women's identity should not be synonymous with "sexual harassment victims." Gage feels that this viewpoint continues to reinforce a negative opinion of women and their powerlessness. It cements the ideology that men are strong, and women are weak. Her focus is on self-responsibility, independence, and autonomy. Groups embracing helplessness and victimhood perpetuate women's suffering and abuse.[79] "My issue is how the conversation is happening. And my issue is also about being dragged into the conversation purely based on gender."[80]

Similarly, Gage reported that Morgan Freeman, an American actor, and film narrator, despises the "black" conversation. In an earlier interview with Mike Wallace, who was an American journalist, Freeman stated that he did not want

69

a black history month. "Black History Month," the month of February, is an annual observance in the United States to remember important people and events in the history of the African diaspora. Freeman felt that history is American history. He wanted people to stop talking about racism. He stated that he would no longer call Mike Wallace, "a white man," and he did not want Mike Wallace to refer to him as "a black man." They were both "American!" We will never get rid of discrimination if we keep labeling people as white, black, brown gay, etc. Other than physical descriptions, that reference has no substance.

The issue of abusive behavior and the subsequent consequences has only come to the forefront of our society within the last decade. It has become politically correct to expose all perpetrators, no matter how far back the transgressions occurred. However, the social norms and behaviors in American society from decades ago were not judged as unacceptable and grievous at that time. As a society, we must be open to the viewpoint that we cannot punish individuals' offenses based on today's standards of respect and morality. We need to learn from our past, understand the norms of society today, and teach each generation respect and dignity for one another, whether the person is a male or female, black or white, or of any religious denomination. This is the same scenario played out today with people tearing down statues and defacing monuments in the "Black Lives Matter" movement. George Washington was a slave owner, but by the standards of his era, that was not a problem. Judging him and many others by the standards of the 21st century is unfair and unproductive.

Gage reminds us that secure people do not shout about being secure. Happy people don't need to talk about being happy. Strong people do not go around talking about how strong they are. In her opinion, self-help does not improve people's lives. Mark Manson, an American self-help author, blogger, and entrepreneur, stated: "Self-help reinforces perceptions of inferiority and shame. A lot of women's movements are at this same risk."[81] The more you focus on an idea, the more you cement it. We do not control other people's behaviors. We can only control our behavior. Many people find themselves in toxic relationships and waste time trying to negotiate with their partner, hanging around for years. They are waiting for them to improve. And in the meantime, they are telling themselves, "Everything would be so wonderful if only their partners would change." They are yelling and crying at their partners in frustration and anger. That is not the solution. The only people we control are ourselves. So rather than focusing on what we wish everyone else would do differently, we would experience more personal growth if we directed all this energy onto ourselves.

Today, many people and groups embrace the psychology of helplessness and victimhood. They prefer to explain all their difficulties and struggles in terms of the actions of others. There is now a growing appreciation in our culture, of the importance of self-reliance, the need to take destiny into our own hands. "Who is to blame" is a waste of time that detracts from resolution and moving forward. One thing is clear. Women should not have to teach men, not to sexually assault and harass them. Nobody should have to teach anybody not to abuse them.

Although not as often, it happens to men as well, especially gay men. In today's political climate, men who are being accused, face investigations to determine if their actions were a crime, a civil violation, or sordid behavior.

Abuse is often perpetrated by men who are threatened by other men. They feel vulnerable and lash out at individuals whom they think they can control. Women feel devalued in a patriarchal society. Men need to reflect, be humble, and admit fault for their past transgressions. Men must develop their independence and not feel threatened by women. As a society, we need to redefine healthy masculinity that is no better or worse than femininity, but as opposites, are equal. We alone control our behavior. Self-reliance and personal responsibility demonstrate our ability to direct our destiny. Our energy must be focused on how we can succeed and live a fully productive life.

> *"In the long run, we shape our lives, and we shape ourselves. The process never ends until we die. And the choices we make are our responsibility."*[82]
>
> *Eleanor Roosevelt*

The #MeToo Movement

The #MeToo Movement focuses on the sexual misconduct of men in recent times. The movement was founded in 2006 by Tarana Burke to help survivors of sexual violence, particularly women of color from low-income families, to find help to deal with the abuse.[83] On Sunday, October 15, 2017, Alyssa Milano, an actress, invited women to respond to her tweet about #MeToo if you experienced sexual harassment or assault. The response on social media was overwhelming, with over 19 million tweets a year later from around the world.[84] "Amid the firestorm that ignited, some women of color noted that the longtime effort of Ms. Burke, who is black, had not received support over the years from prominent white feminists."[85] Tarana Burke's vision was to make available both information and resources for survivors to stop sexual abuse in their communities with the help of other women who had gone through similar trauma. The #MeToo Movement has become global now, involving women from all walks of life. It has helped women to come forward without feeling the stigma. All concerned citizens want to try to disrupt the systems that perpetuate abuse from continuing. They want to include all the people who have been abused: children, men, women, gay individuals, transgender people, disabled individuals, and people of all color. They hope that there will be a long-term change in our societies and that the perpetrators will be held accountable. A Canadian author tweeted and echoed the cries of so many: "And I was blamed for it. I was told not to talk about

it. I was told that it was not that bad. I was told to get over it."
Najwa Zebian[86]

Recently, hundreds of powerful people, including celebrities, politicians, and CEOs have been accused of sexual harassment or assault allegations. Since April 2017, there is a list of over 263 individuals accused of crimes and misdemeanors related to sexual abuse.[87] Most of the women coming forward feel comfortable speaking up because of the others who have come before them. Some are reporting abuse from many years ago, while others, more recently. It is a legal problem. There is no proof in the eyes of the law, determining who was victimized, and who just wants their five minutes of fame. After all, in a court of law, a judge will give the jury explicit instructions. "There must be a fair and thorough consideration of evidence or lack thereof, or all persons are presumed innocent, and no person may be convicted of an offense unless each element of the offense is proved beyond a reasonable doubt."[88]

In the case of impeachment against President Bill Clinton for lying under oath, there was the infamous blue dress of Monica Lewinsky.[89] Despite the "proof" of sexual activity confirmed by the FBI in the case, the country was very forgiving. Bill Clinton continued to serve out his presidency and remained popular. Women should have realized that powerful men would take advantage of them. However, as noted previously, Monica Lewinsky admitted it was a consensual relationship, even if misguided. In the past, they must have been more forgiving, less concerned about extra-marital affairs and lying about them. Throughout the years and even today in our culture, powerful men have been known to have multiple affairs while married. It should not be a surprise to anyone that these transgressions still occur.

In reviewing the list of complaints and charges by women in the #MeToo Movement, every woman should be able to stand up and say that they have been sexually harassed. And every man should take ownership that they have offended some woman in their lifetime. The only thing that men can do is apologize for their past behaviors. Mistakes and ownership of those wrongdoings have the power to turn you into something better than you were before as a person. The only thing that abused women can do is to accept those apologies for the men's past behaviors. Everyone needs to stop focusing on the past and move forward. Memories can be harrowingly painful. They remind us of a time when we were deeply wounded emotionally. Sadly, those experiences were part of your life. To move on, one must be able to accept the past that cannot be changed, forgive the individuals who have caused the pain, and look to the future. By forgiving those individuals, you are releasing yourself from the anger and hurt from past events. Only you can have different expectations for your future.

Men display many forms of sexual behavior. While women are walking past them, they may whistle. Some men make comments or even initiate unwanted advances. Some men are bold enough to pat a woman on the butt or look down her blouse that reveals the top of her breasts. Why do women purposefully dress to attract men's attention to their breasts, legs, or other body parts? Then women get upset when men or women look at them. Some men take a provocative dress as an invitation. Women want to be noticed but complain when they are noticed. Men read more into this appearance than intended. It is a difficult situation. It should be a shared responsibility. While traveling to work, at the office, or a party especially when alcohol loosens up inhibitions, men may try to touch a woman. Bolder men will point to their engorged penis and press themselves against a woman. And some men, who are the most daring, will push themselves further onto a woman and may rape her.

Many women have complained of psychological intimidation at the workplace where they felt that they had to have sex with their bosses to keep their jobs, receive an excellent evaluation, or obtain a promotion or a raise in salary. Young girls are particularly vulnerable in their teens and twenties while they are traveling alone. Older men tend to be friendly and protective, but then they make their moves. Unless the young women are confident to realize what is happening, they can be taken advantage of sexually.

Is this the norm for society? Do women have to just shrug off this unwanted sexual behavior by men? Is it men's DNA make-up to behave in this manner towards women? Is it more difficult for men to control their social behavior? Psychological research has determined "insecure men in positions of power would be more likely to engage in sexual harassment behaviors. Fears of incompetence lead to abuse of subordinates, presumably to restore social status, and alleviate negative, highly unpleasant, and even unacceptable self-perceptions."[90] Some women suffering from sexual abuse seek professional psychological help to accept what has happened to them and to learn how to heal emotionally from the traumatic experience. Other women cry foul at the slightest hint of any sexual innuendo. Today, sexual harassment, abuse, and any form of intimidation are at their highest point in public awareness. The news continues to assault our senses with new revelations by men accused of these potential crimes.

It is reasonable to say that our sensitivity level about sexual harassment crimes and misdemeanors is quite different from twenty to fifty years ago. During the 1960s and 1970s, the "Hippie Days," there was a counterculture movement, originating on college campuses. It was in part opposition to the United States' involvement in the Vietnam War. Many young people felt alienated from middle-class society and decided to drop out of school. They advocated living together in communes, often practiced open sexual relationships, and usage of hallucinogenic drugs, like marijuana and LSD. They supported music festivals like Woodstock, a three-day gathering of close to half a million young people in 1969. They sought spiritual guidance from eastern religions like Buddhism.[91] American cities were inundated with thousands of young people participating in sit-ins, protesting the war, and other social injustices within American society. They became a subculture that rocked America and changed the world.

The changes in sexual attitudes and behavior in American culture were paramount at this time. Sex became more socially acceptable outside the strict confines of heterosexual marriage. The social and political climate of the 60s was one of profound change. Young people protested and challenged dramatically previously accepted societal norms.[92] Liberalism, a drive for civil liberty and equality for all, full support for social justice and a mixed economy (means of production are shared between private and public sectors) in all aspects of American life, became a driving force.

Today, sexual harassment or unwelcome sexual advances, requests for sexual favors, or other verbal or physical harassment are unlawful, whether the victim or the harasser be either male or female. However, according to the U.S. Equal Employment Opportunity Commission, the deadline time limits for filing a complaint through the EEOC charge is either 180 days or 300 days after the last date of the alleged harassment, depending on the state in which the allegation arises. Time is an essential factor when determining to pursue legal proceedings of sexual harassment in every state. In the State of New York, an individual will be charged with first- degree rape, when this person engages in sexual intercourse with another person by forcible compulsion, with a physically helpless individual, with a child less than eleven years old, or with a child less than thirteen years old and the accused is at least eighteen years old. There is no time limit to commence a criminal action against the perpetrator.[93] In September 2019, New York Governor Andrew Cuomo signed into law legislation that extends the statute of limitations for some cases of rape and other sex crimes. "Under the new law, the statute for reporting second- degree rape increases to 20 years and third-degree rape to 10 years. Previously, both were five years. Times have changed drastically across the country about the litigation of sexual crimes."[94]

Yet, on the opposite side of a sexual dispute, there are women like Stormy Daniels, a pornographic actress, stripper, screenwriter, and director who wants the world to know that she had sex with the President of the United States, Donald Trump. Not only did she get paid for her services, but she also realized how much more money she could receive by advertising her exploits and adding to the sexual harassment news. It is difficult to feel sorry for her and believe that she was taken advantage of unfairly. She seems to want to set the record straight. She has not revealed to the media how much money she has earned from publicizing her sexual exploits. She has stated that her reputation is tarnished, although she is a pornographic actress who works in adult films.[95]

A significant amount of information has been written about role modeling and how men are supposed to behave. Women need to be held to the same high standards also. Women need to demonstrate some tolerance and show strength to put a stop to sexual harassment. Both men and women together must become more active in teaching younger children how to be respectful to all individuals, in addition to instructing children how to recognize physical and sexual abuses. We, as a society, need to move forward. Rehashing the sexual mores of the past is not productive. Another story posted with the #MeToo Movement is not going to create the societal change that we so desperately need today to give dignity and respect to every human being, no matter their age, gender, sex, or origin.

Men Accused of Sexual Misconduct

A long list exists, of men who have been accused of sexual harassment. Sadly, their reputations have been destroyed beyond repair. However, many of these men also made contributions to society that will be erased. Nikki M. Taylor, a historian at Howard University, stated: "Good historians also must be able to see and write about the bad in good people and the good in bad people. In short, we must be able to write about humanity in both our heroes and villains."[96]

William James O'Reilly, Jr., born in 1949, is an American journalist, author, and was a television host. He had been working with television stations since the late 1970s. He joined Fox News channel in 1996 and hosted "The O'Reilly Factor" until 2017 when he was fired for numerous allegations of sexual harassment over many years. Media analyst Howard Kurtz described him as "the biggest star in the 20-year history at Fox News" at the time of his departure.[97] "'The O'Reilly Factor' spent fifteen years as the highest-rated cable news show. Other analysts said that it brought in $325 million in ad revenue in 2015 – 2016 alone, making it the top revenue producer of any show on Fox News, CNN, or MSNBC."[98] His career took a major blow after various New York Times investigations reported that he had paid out over $50 million to a dozen women to settle multiple sexual harassment lawsuits. Lis Wiehl, a former Fox News analyst, reportedly received a $32 million settlement where she says, "O'Reilly initiated a non-consensual sexual relationship with her."[99]

Readers need to come to their own conclusions about this information. Many questions remain about the perpetrators and their accusers. Did Bill O'Reilly and other men settle their cases to avoid negative publicity? Why didn't these women speak up sooner? Why would women participate in non-consensual sex? Why didn't they resign from their positions? Were all these women so fearful and intimidated? Or were they more interested in punishing a harsh, overbearing individual and receiving a windfall of millions of dollars, more than they would ever earn in their lifetimes? Today, these women should think seriously about their participation in this employment debacle, to have consensual sex to save their jobs. They must examine why they would choose to be victims instead of stopping the abuse from taking place in the first place.

Over the past century, few entertainers, let alone a Black male had achieved the success and legendary status of William H. Cosby, Jr. His success spans five decades and encompasses all forms of media. Bill Cosby came from very humble beginnings, growing up in a Philadelphia project. In the 1960s, his stand-up act was a great success that created best-selling comedy albums. He went on to win eight Gold Records, five Platinum Records, and five Grammy Awards. His role in "I Spy" made him the first African American to co-star in a dramatic series. His character helped to break television's racial barrier, and he won three Emmy Awards. In the 1980s, "The Cosby Show" was a top-rated sitcom that the whole family could enjoy about the Huxtable family. He starred in hit movies like "Uptown Saturday Night." He wrote best-selling books one entitled "Fatherhood." He had a fantastic ability to touch people's hearts.

His main message to young black males was to take responsibility for their children. He felt that they needed to work hard, be responsible, and take care of their families. Single mothers raise many African American children. 57.6% of black children, 31.2% of Hispanic children, and 20.7% of white children are living in homes without their biological fathers.[100] He often spoke about black people focusing on the fact that they were black and using the race card.

Shockingly, in April 2018, Bill Cosby was found guilty of three counts of aggravated indecent assault for drugging and sexually assaulting Andrea Constand at his home in a Philadelphia suburb in 2004. The 80-year-old comedian was sentenced to ten years in jail. This verdict came a year after Cosby's previous trial ended in a mistrial. At the retrial, five other Cosby accusers testified that he had drugged and assaulted them decades ago. This trial was the first notable celebrity sexual assault trial since the #MeToo Movement began in 2017. Many people wondered if similar cases would end up in court. The Montgomery County District Attorney Kevin Steele told reporters "Cosby used his celebrity, wealth, network of supporters to conceal his crimes."[101] Cosby's attorney, Tom Mesereau, said he plans to fight the verdict and appeal very strongly. "We do not think that Mr. Cosby is guilty of anything, and the fight is not over."[102] During the trial there was the "he said, she said" dynamic that is common to sexual assault trials. There was little forensic evidence.

No one other than the two people know the truth. With the current sentimentality, people want to believe the women involved in these cases because of the outrageous behaviors that men have displayed. Other than the women feeling vindicated if these incidents did occur, what other satisfaction did they derive from sending an 80-year-old man to prison and ruining his reputation and life's work? Are we to forget and minimize all the good that he had also accomplished in his lifetime? Sadly, notorious acts are always remembered more than worthy causes. If these women go after Cosby for monetary damages or sign book deals, earn fees through interviews, perhaps we have an answer to their pursuit of celebrity and fame.

Without absolute proof as to what happened, trigger-happy reactions are already taking place all over the country, going back decades to prove sexual harassment cases. These events may be happening to show support and be more sensitive to women in the #MeToo Movement. Sadly, hours after the verdict, Carnegie Mellon University in Pittsburgh, Pennsylvania, announced it was revoking the honorary degree it had bestowed on Cosby in 2007. The University of Notre Dame in South Bend, Indiana, also announced it was rescinding the honorary degree it awarded to Cosby in 1990.[103] However, Temple University, where Cosby attended college, stated the verdict "provides additional facts for the university to consider concerning Bill Cosby's honorary degree and respects the jury's decision." In 2014, Cosby had resigned from Temple's Board of Trustees after holding a seat for 32 years.[104] Hollywood had to do their part. Bill Cosby was expelled from the Academy of Motion Picture Arts and Sciences in keeping with the group's new ethical conduct rules.[105]

The question now remains to be answered about how far back people are going to go to dig up infractions and make accusations against men without any forensic proof. No matter how long ago or how old men are, will we seek justice, and to what end? These legal cases have been mainly about men's sexual transgressions until now. Melanie Martinez, a singer, and songwriter was the only woman to be placed on the list of sexual predators for "raping" a singer, Timothy Heller. He stated: "I never said: 'Yes!' I said: 'No', repeatedly! But she used her power over me and broke me down."[106]

In August 2018, an Italian actress, Asia Argento, one of the leading voices of the #MeToo Movement, was in a situation where she needed to defend herself.[107] She had denied the allegations that she had a sexual relationship with the young actor when he was seventeen years old. She reported that they were "absolutely false," although there were reports that she texted her friends stating that she did not know he was underage![108] The New York Times reported that Argento, aged 42, settled allegations about a notice of intent to sue sent by Jimmy Bennett, aged 22 now, for $380,000. This revelation came about a few months after she accused Harvey Weinstein of rape.[109] Argento claimed that her boyfriend, Anthony Bourdain, made the payment to Jimmy Bennett due to his severe financial problems. "Anthony personally undertook to benefit Bennett economically, upon the condition that he would no longer suffer any intrusions in our life."[110] Perhaps, over time, all men and women will have the courage to speak up honestly and admit their own transgressions.

Casey Affleck had sexual harassment allegations made against him, which forced him to avoid participating in the 2018 Oscars' ceremony.[111] As the winner of the Best Actor award for

Manchester by the Sea the previous year, he was scheduled to present the Best Actress award. The allegations against him stemmed from a pair of sexual harassment suits he faced while directing the 2010 Joaquin Phoenix quasi-documentary *I'm Still Here*.[112] Although Affleck denied any wrongdoing, he ultimately settled both lawsuits. He would have liked to resolve things differently. Affleck had never received any complaint of sexual harassment made against him. It was embarrassing, and he did not know how to handle the complaints. He did not agree with everything, the way it was described, and what the accusers were saying about him. Affleck wanted to try and put the accusations behind him and move on with his life. He settled the legal suits in a manner that was asked of him at the time.[113]

The number of men and women accused of sexual harassment, sexual assault, and casual sexual offenses grows daily. Is the real purpose of the #MeToo Movement to stop further attacks from happening or to ruin the reputations of people who have contributed to society? Years later, can possible infractions cause their demise? Some celebrities have chosen to not even challenge the accusations, despite allegations made against them, sometimes by anonymous individuals. How are individuals able to say these things without proof, and how do we know who is telling the truth? Who is just seeking their five minutes of fame? What recourse do men and women have when allegations are made against them without any substantial proof?

"A standard of proof refers to the person responsible for proving the case. There are different standards of proof in different circumstances. The three primary standards of proof are proof beyond a reasonable doubt, a preponderance of the evidence, and clear and convincing evidence. A preponderance of evidence is the lowest standard of evidence. It means that it is more likely than not that the facts are what one party claims. Clear and convincing evidence is a step up from a preponderance of the evidence. This standard shows that it is highly probable or probably certain that the thing alleged has occurred. Proof beyond a reasonable doubt is the standard of proof in criminal prosecutions. The prosecutor has the duty to convince the jury by proof beyond a reasonable doubt of each and every element of the crime before a jury could convict a defendant."[114]

Harvey Weinstein, co-founder and film producer of the entertainment company Miramax, was fired from the company after more than eighty women reported that he had sexually harassed or assaulted them or raped them, involving incidents dating back decades ago.[115] One must question and wonder why so many women put up with this behavior before taking responsibility to put a stop to this behavior by one man. These women have fathers, husbands, boyfriends, and male friends to confide in and to ask for assistance. The only way these women can resolve this abuse is NOT to let this behavior continue. Making accusations and pointing fingers may not stop these men who are determined to play the power game and take advantage of them. The women themselves must set up clear boundaries and expectations in their relationships with men. They may have to walk away from job opportunities with these individuals and recognize these individuals for what they are. Their self-esteem and self-preservation are more valuable than any paycheck.

Matt Lauer, a former news anchor for NBC and co-host of the Today Show, was fired after multiple women reported that he sexually harassed or assaulted them.[116] A former producer stated: "He couldn't sleep around town with celebrities or on the road with random people, because he's Matt Lauer and married. So, he had to do it within his stable, where he exerted power, and he knew people would never complain."[117] The question to be pondered is why these grown women did not complain. After all, they knew what he was doing was wrong. The NBC organization fired him. What was happening inside the organization before the #MeToo Movement?

Tom Brokaw was recently accused of sexual harassment. Former NBC correspondent Linda Vester and another woman stated that Brokaw sexually harassed them in the 1990s. Brokaw, now in his 70s, vehemently denies these claims.[118] More than sixty of his colleagues, including Maria Shiver, Rachel Maddow, and Andrea Mitchell, wrote a letter defending him as a man of "tremendous dignity and integrity."[119] A third woman claimed that he made unwanted sexual advances towards her fifty years ago! He has denied any wrongdoing.

Why does anyone hold onto these memories for 50 years? Things done in the past when people were young, and single would be considered taboo today. However, these behaviors were acceptable back then within one's circle of friends. Social norms and behavioral standards change, and people need to acknowledge this fact.

The value of a good reputation is indisputable. "Your reputation lives an authentic existence apart from you, representing the collective mental construct everyone but you, shares about you, a construct based partially on your actions but also on the perceptions others have about other's perceptions of your actions."[120] It is so easy to destroy one's reputation with false accusations. Men seem to be paralyzed with the prospect of trying to maintain their hard-earned reputation. All they can say after being charged with allegations is: "it did not happen" or "I do not remember it that way." Just because more than one woman accused the same man, does that make the accusations verifiable?

This silence may be the reason why many men are not speaking up to defend themselves as they have no recourse to prove their innocence. The women who are making these allegations need to have proof to back up their allegations, to make them legitimate. Otherwise, please think carefully before tarnishing someone's reputation forever. It appears that many women want to be noticed by the media, which is hungry for these accusations to surface and sensationalize these events to attract a larger viewing audience. The expression *"Hell has no fury like a woman scorned"* did not come into existence without some truth to the statement.[121] Women are more emotional and can be vindictive. Men can be ruthless in business and their drive for power, but they also tend to keep their feelings bottled up. They are not very vocal even when it might help their cause to be more outspoken. Men are not very adept at dealing with their emotions and many do not know what to say or do, even when it is necessary to defend themselves.

An investigation performed by the former FBI director Louis Freeh in July 2012 concluded that Joseph Vincent Paterno had concealed information relating to his former defensive coordinator, Gerald Sandusky's abuse of young boys.[122] A critique of the Freeh report by the law firm of King & Spalding and expert opinion from the former U.S. Attorney General and Pennsylvania Governor Dick Thornburgh, among others, disputed Paterno's involvement in the alleged cover-up. "It was determined that the report was deeply flawed and that key conclusions regarding Joe Paterno were unsubstantiated and unfair."[123]

The way Paterno was railroaded would give anyone pause to think about forgiveness and the concept of "throwing the baby out with the bathwater," which means avoiding an obvious error in judgment when something or someone was good when trying to eliminate what or who was bad at the same time.[124] He was the head coach of the Penn State Nittany Lions from 1966 to 2011. With 409 victories, Paterno is the most victorious coach in NCAA FBS history. He recorded his 409th victory on October 29, 2011. His career ended 11 days later with his dismissal from the team on November 9, 2011, as a result of the Penn State child abuse scandal. He died 74 days later, on January 22, 2012, of complications from lung cancer.[125]

After the child abuse scandal broke in November 2011, Paterno announced that he would retire at the end of the season. However, on November 9, the Penn State Board of Trustees rejected his offer and immediately terminated his contract. On July 23, 2012, the NCAA vacated all of Penn State's wins from 1998 through 2011 as part of the punishment for the child abuse scandal. The association eliminated 111 of the games that Paterno had coached and won, which dropped him from 1st to 12th on the list of winningest NCAA football coaches. In January 2013, a lawsuit was launched against the NCAA, and as part of the settlement, the NCAA reversed its decision on

January 16, 2015, and restored the 111 wins to Paterno's record.[126]

Here was a man who coached his team to five undefeated seasons in (1968, 1969, 1973, 1984, 1986). The team won two national championships in 1982 and 1986. He coached five undefeated teams that won major bowl games, and in 2007 was inducted into the College Football Hall of Fame as a coach. He chose to stay with the Nittany Lions and turned down offers to coach National Football League teams, including the Pittsburg Steelers and the New England Patriots.[127]

Despite the 61 years of dedication to his players and loyalty to Penn State University, Paterno died with the shame of being fired from his coaching career. He had not committed any acts of abuse himself but was punished, nonetheless. His family may have felt vindicated with the NCAA decision reversal in 2015, but Paterno died feeling all the good he had done during his lifetime was washed away by a knee-jerk reaction by the Penn State Board of Trustees. They insisted on punishing the entire staff in the football program at Penn State.

Gerald Sandusky, an assistant coach under Paterno, who founded "The Second Mile," a non- profit charity serving Pennsylvania's underprivileged and at-risk youth at Penn State University, was arrested, and charged with 52 counts of sexual abuse. He was found guilty of 45 charges and sent to prison for 30 to 60 years, which is a life sentence. He got what he deserved, but also destroyed the careers of many other professionals.[128]

And it is still difficult to understand the sharp fall from grace and resignation from the US Senate by Senator Al Franken. He is an American comedian, writer, producer, and politician, who served as a Senator from Minnesota from 2009 until 2018. He had to step down from his seat amongst sexual allegations against him, another victim of the #MeToo Movement. "Leeann Tweeden, a conservative talk-radio host, accused him of forcing an unwanted kiss on her during a 2006 USO tour. Seven more women followed with accusations against Franken of inappropriate touches and kisses."[129] Franken commented, "that being on the losing side of the #MeToo Movement, which he fervently supports, has led him to spend time thinking about such matters as due process, the proportionality of punishment, and the consequences of Internet-fueled outrage."[130]

John Ziegler, a Mediaite columnist, defended Al Franken and thought he was unjustly treated in the media. He wrote "it sure feels like Franken is getting railroaded and that much of the issue revolves around context and Tweeden's current profession. Tweeden working as a news anchor, gives her a clear incentive to exaggerate her story for publicity."[131] She posted her story on her news station website, which gave it validity. However, it was her version of the event.

It has been verified that the incident occurred during a comedy sketch rehearsal during which Franken delivered the highly inappropriate kiss. Franken had been performing the same sketch at previous USO events with different women. The comedian did not write the kiss into the scene to target Tweeden, as she alleged. Tweeden was still angry 12 years later about what Franken did to her. It is unclear why she did not speak up at the time. The photo of Franken posing in 2006, while appearing to grope Tweeden, who was protected by a military-grade flak jacket, can be very misleading, cutting out the moments before and after from the record that could completely change our perception of what happened. It is not clear if he was groping a flak jacket for comedic effect or sexual gratification.

When Franken ran for the US Senate in 2007, just a couple of months after the groping photo was taken, Tweeden did not speak up or report any allegations against Franken. And in 2017, after accusing Franken of sexual misconduct, 36 SNL women, former scriptwriters, production assistants, and cast members, including Jane Curtin and Laraine Newman, signed an open letter defending their former colleague. They stated, "We feel compelled to stand up for Al Franken, whom we have all had the pleasure of working with over the years on Saturday Night Live. What Al did was stupid and foolish, and we think it was appropriate to apologize to Ms. Tweeden and the public. In our experience, we know Al as a devoted and dedicated family man, a wonderful comedic performer, and an honorable public servant. That is why we are moved to quickly and directly affirm that after years of working with him, we would like to acknowledge that not one of us ever experienced any inappropriate behavior and mention our sincere appreciation that he treated us with the utmost respect and regard."[132]

Senator Amy Klobuchar said that she expected Franken to remain in the Senate. She did not join other Democrats who called for Franken to step down in December 2017. Despite criticism from some individuals that Franken had been forced out, Klobuchar stated that Franken had chosen to resign. He felt that the accusations against him would make it exceedingly difficult to do his job in the Senate. Franken did state that some of the allegations he faced were not true, while others stemmed from interactions that he remembered very differently.[133]

Women senators in the US Senate mainly led the charge for Franken to resign. However, soon they were joined by dozens of Democrats, men, and women alike, including Senate Minority Leader Chuck Schumer. In his words, "I consider Senator Franken, a dear friend and greatly respect his accomplishments, but he has an obligation to his constituents and the Senate and should step down immediately."[134] The senators in the US Senate did not demonstrate the spirit of the law and the due process of the law about the case against Senator Al Franken. There was a rush to judgment, a herd mentality, wanting to do what was culturally accessible at the time, instead of following Senate procedures for due process and graduated sanctions.

In an online interview, Jane Mayer, a leading journalist, who has been reporting on sexual assault and harassment allegations, informed Terry Gross, and the audience "the story told by Franken's chief accuser Leeann Tweeden was full of holes."[135] Mayer investigated the allegations against Franken thoroughly. She interviewed his senate staff, former comedians on SNL, other women who came forward with accusations, and even the lawyer, Debbie Katz, who represented Christine Blasey Ford, the woman who accused Justice Kavanaugh of sexual misbehavior many years ago. She concluded "all accused individuals deserve due process and that there is proportionality in terms of being able to distinguish different gradations of bad behavior. Not everybody is Harvey Weinstein, but there may be other kinds of misconduct that also need to be addressed, but in different ways."

If the accused person is famous, then almost any allegation, no matter how old it is, seems purely on its own, to be fair game. While there is a positive side to accusers now being given so much instant credibility, not all allegations are true, just as there may be some truth behind some denials of misconduct. Some men are pretending that these experiences did not happen. Men are uncharacteristically quiet with the #MeToo Movement. Their silence may be from the fear of being the next one to be attacked in the media. Unfortunately, they are gaslighting women with their silence.

The need for a dose of skepticism is particularly urgent as men who have apologized for their indiscretions are not given any opportunity to continue to perform the excellent work that they have done throughout their careers. With all the negative publicity, they have to resign or face continued bombardment to their reputation and dignity. They lose all respect because someone said something, and it must be true, especially if more than one woman has made accusations. They are forced into hiding and seclusion.

Does anyone stop to think that there may be reasons for these allegations? One can think of several. Women who have felt that men, especially in powerful positions, have taken advantage of them, and this is a way for the women to retaliate. The women may have been abused by someone else and have carried that anger for years. Now there is an opportunity to get back at men in general. They falsely accuse someone, and the media runs with the story, without much verification or reporting the accounts of both sides of the story. Many men who have contributed to society throughout their lives are losing their career, reputation, respect in society, only to be remembered because someone felt violated by a touch, comment, or suggestion.

Women need to be better than that. Sexual harassment must stop, but it will only end when women speak up at the time when incidents occur. Women need to come forward through the appropriate channels, not the media! Do not drudge up issues years later when there is no proof of what happened or whose memory is more accurate or less tainted with other events from the past. How many of us can accurately remember all events from the past and describe them with absolute certainty? False memories are embedded within all of us. We all have arguments when one person remembers the event in one way while another involved may retain the memory of the same situation differently. Emotions affect how memories are stored in the brain.

> *"Just because someone thinks they remember something in detail, with confidence and emotion, does not mean that it actually happened. False memories have these characteristics too. With our independent corroboration, little can be done to tell a false memory from a true one."*[136]
>
> *Elizabeth Loftus*

Part 3

Moving Forward

An Historical Perspective

From the Bible in the Book of Genesis, there are three clear pictures that emerge about women. The first one depicts the story of how women were created. Adam's words when presented with Eve: "This is now bone of my bone, and flesh of my flesh: she shall be called woman because she was taken out of man." Genesis 2:23[137] Woman was supposedly created from the rib of a man, but it takes both male and female to bear God's image. The second picture is the temptation and the fall. Eve was the seductress who enticed Adam to eat the fruit and corrupted him. "She took of the fruit and ate thereof. She also gave unto her husband with her, and he did eat." Genesis 3:6[138] Given free will, both man and woman make disastrous choices with stunning consequences. However, both Adam and Eve were eligible for forgiveness. And in the third picture, women are of equal worth in heaven, standing shoulder to shoulder praising God.

Dr. Sarah Sumner cites in her book: *Men and Women in the Church: Building Consensus on Church Leadership,* that there are several expressions of deep prejudice against women in the writings of the church fathers.[139] Church leaders did not often teach the potential equality between men and women as implied in Jesus' message. Tertullian, an early author, and influential teacher from the third century, living in Carthage, what is now the country of Tunisia in Africa, was the first Christian author to produce a significant body of work on Latin Christian literature. The idea of the "Trinity" originated with Tertullian. He defined the "Trinity" as the Father, Son, and Holy

Spirit.[140] He compared all women to Eve, calling them "the devil's gateway, the unsealed of that forbidden tree and she who persuaded him, the devil was not vigilant enough to attack."[141] Tertullian's viewpoint went even further, declaring that women were the root of all evil. He argued that Eve and therefore all of womankind, "God's image man, was condemned to death, and that the Son of God himself had to come to die."[142]

Augustine, probably the most famous theologian in all of church history, believed that God only created women for procreation. "If it were not the case that the woman was created to be man's helper specifically for the production of children, then why would she have been created as 'helper'?"(Gen.2:18)[143] He was born November 13, 354 AD, and an early Christian doctor of the church, a Roman African, and the bishop of Hippo Regius in North Africa.[144] He also expressed the ease of two men living together: "How much more it is for two friends to eat, drink, and talk together than for a man and woman to dwell together."[145]

In the Middle Ages, the role of the woman was to marry and bear children. Amongst the elite, parents often arranged or forced marriage on their daughters. However, during the time of persecution, when men were getting killed, women were able to hold important positions and climbed the social ladder in the church and society. "The Roman government under emperor Nero in 64 AD ordered persecutions of Christians in the early church. The total number of those who lost their lives is unknown, but the early church historian, Eusebius, spoke of great multitudes, who perished."[146] Once the males returned from battle, they continued to dominate the society, and women were again knocked down the social ladder.

Since ancient times, women have been used for the satisfaction of men. Every culture has left behind evidence of men going to women to get their sexual urges satisfied in brothels, whore houses and dance halls. It is also an uncomfortable part of the U.S. military's long history with prostitution. The world's oldest profession has long catered to U.S. troops, whether at home or abroad.[147] In World War II, posters warned U.S. soldiers in Europe that "you can't beat the Axis if you get VD." Things may have been even worse in Japan, where American officials allowed an official brothel system for the use of U.S. troops until 1946, when Gen. Douglas MacArthur shut it down. During Vietnam War, prostitution was common. Infamously depicted in the 1987 movie "Full Metal Jacket," it played a role in creating a generation of half-Americans in Vietnam who are now mostly in their 40s, according to a Global Post report in 2011.

Today, in gentlemen's clubs, the only difference is that young women can work in these establishments for a few hours every week and earn good money to fund their education and further their career choice. The new-age way is to sign up and offer one's services through "sugar-daddy.com."

In the oldest civilizations like India, females have always been treated as being less worthy than men. During the late 18th century in India, there were still elaborate rituals and strict moral codes. There were ancient traditions such as child marriage (Gouridaan), polygamy (the practice of having more than one wife at a time), and the practice of self-immolation of widows, setting oneself on fire at their husband's funeral pyre (Sati Pratha), so as not to burden her in- laws or society.[148] "Young women were married to much older men, in return for a dowry."[149] Raja Ram Mohan Roy, who was a social and educational reformer, contributed immensely to eradicating those prevalent social evils and traditions in Indian society in the 18th century. He was a highly educated and religious individual who sought to integrate Western culture with the best customs of his own country. He worked diligently to promote a modern system of education from a Sanskrit education to an English-based one.[150] All of his life, he was focused on changing the social injustices that plagued Indian culture, especially those against women.

In the 19th century and throughout the 20th century, India was mainly an agrarian society. Male children were needed in the fields to plant and harvest the crops. Female children were not considered to be able to work as hard as male children. Fathers had to provide a dowry for their female children to marry. "The dowry system in India refers to the durable goods, cash, real or movable property that the bride's family gives to the bridegroom, his parents, or his relatives as a condition of the marriage. It put an extreme financial burden on the bride's family. In many cases, it led to crimes against women, from emotional abuse to even death. The payment of a dowry has been prohibited since the Dowry Prohibition Act of 1961 and the Indian Penal Code. Although the law has been effective for over sixty years in India, the practice of the dowry is still evident in many parts of India."[151] Dowry is disguised as wedding gifts. For many years, the financial burden was so difficult for families that female babies were killed at birth, female genocide. "According to women's rights activist, Donna Fernandes, some practices are so deeply embedded within Indian culture that it is almost impossible to do away with them. In 2012, the United Nations declared that female children in India between the ages of one and five were more likely to die than male children."[152] Although this practice has decreased throughout India, there is a surplus of men and not enough women of the marrying age.

In the past, Indian women did not have access to educational opportunities. Their only role in life was to bear children, cook, clean, take care of the men, and other family members. Females received the blame for not being able to bear sons, even though the man anatomically decides the gender of the baby. "Men determine the sex of a baby, depending on whether the sperm is carrying an X or Y chromosome. An 'X' chromosome combines with the mother's 'X' chromosome to make a baby girl (XX). A 'Y' chromosome will connect with the mother's to make a boy (XY)."[153]

The rules of society are changing for females in India. More young women are attending college. "A 2018 educational report prepared by All India Survey of Higher Education (AISHA) revealed that the number of women in college increased 1,350% over seven years from 2011 to 2018. However, in the same year, the World Bank Report on Labor Force Participation, only 29% of women were part of the workforce."[154] Rules are changing within Indian culture, which always centered on family traditions, getting married to bear children, and continuing the family name. The middle class is rising "with a growth rate of 7.5% annually until 2030, according to the analysis performed by the consultancy firm of Bain & Company for the World Economic Forum."[155] The population has increased, and there is an economic boom, especially in the global marketplace. Incomes have risen, along with a tremendous growth rate for the GDP (Gross Domestic Product), of which 60% is domestic private consumption.[156] "GDP is the monetary value of all finished goods and services within a country during a specific period."[157]

Females are refusing to get married at a young age, and some young women are choosing not to marry at all, instead, selecting a life-long career. Divorce rates have increased in India; females are no longer tolerating physical and emotional abuse from married partners or their families. The United Nations' Report entitled "Progress of the World's Women 2019 – 2020: Families in a Changing World" noted that "while non-marriage remains extremely rare in India, the number of divorces has doubled over the past two decades."[158]

Many Indian women in their 40s and older still struggle with husbands who dominate and regulate all aspects of the household. Men rarely help with mundane household chores. They expect their wives to prepare all the daily meals and serve them at a specific time, regardless of how busy they were throughout the day. If the men are working and providing financial security, they feel they are not obligated to assist with the household chores. This behavior pattern is perpetuated with sons who observe the pre-established cultural boundaries. Sons are catered to and not encouraged to perform household chores. They, too, expect their mothers to be fully responsible for maintaining the home and taking care of the family. Some young

Indian men who go to college, become more self-sufficient, and are beginning to understand the importance of a shared partnership with raising a family and maintaining a household.

The previous civilizations did not contribute favorably to the propagation of the human species since incest was prevalent within European and Asian cultures. Much inbreeding still occurs in the Muslim culture, giving rise to a high rate of genetically deformed babies. Indian arranged marriages still expect couples to choose their mates from individuals who have grown up from a particular area or have ancestors from a specific set of villages in India. This arrangement exists even though families are scattered around the world. Today, children are going to college and falling in love with individuals of different ethnicities. Maybe now, we have a chance of evolving a stronger, genetically diverse human race.

When China had instituted the one-child rule, female infanticide was rampant. China's one-child policy was a measure to prevent overpopulation within the country. It is directly related to a country's ability to feed and house all citizens. It was an extreme example of family planning. "It was introduced in 1979 and modified in the mid-1980s to allow rural parents to have a second child if their first-born was a daughter. This policy lasted three more decades before being eliminated at the end of 2015. The policy did allow exceptions for some ethnic minorities."[159] "Unfortunately, even now in China and India alone, an estimated two million baby girls go "missing" each year. They are selectively aborted, killed as newborns, or abandoned and left to die."[160] It is the Chinese custom that male sons will take care of their parents in old age.

"In 2014, China had 33 million more men than women, renewing a long-running controversy over selective abortion. And in 2018, there were around 713 million male inhabitants and 682 million female inhabitants, amounting to 1.4 billion people in total, with 31 million more males in comparison to females."[161] Today, the demographics of a one-child society increase the obligations of either sex to provide for their parents since China does not have an adequate welfare system. Older parents must rely on their children for care and support. With an abundance of males in the society, most of these surplus men live in impoverished rural areas, tending family farms. Female villagers were encouraged to migrate in search of better jobs and husbands.

Now in 2020, there is an estimate of 30 to 40 million men known as "guang gun," bare branches, who will never marry or produce "offshoots" of their own.[162] Conversely, young women today in their 20s and 30s whose parents chose to have them, have become highly- educated but face another type of discrimination. "When it comes to the marriage market in China, educated women are often expected to forget their career objectives and honor those of their parents and prospective husbands. Those who do not comply are known as "sheng nu," or leftover women, a phrase that has connotations of leftover, unwanted food. Chinese women, who are approaching the ages of 25 to 30, fall into this category, with a marriage age expiration date."[163] Today, many Chinese men are marrying foreign brides, women from Vietnam, and Cambodia. The Xinhua News Agency indicates that there are over 100,000 Vietnamese women in China who are married to Chinese men. It is difficult to confirm the number. Many of the women have been smuggled into the country and are not registered with the authorities."[164]

In recent times, love is no longer the primary criteria for a marriage arrangement in China. Couples have become increasingly rational when thinking about choosing a life partner. Individuals are looking for others with a comparable income level and even real estate ownership. Young Chinese men and women are also deciding to become established in their careers before getting married. The marriage age has risen from mid-twenties to the early thirties, especially for young women. Young urban women in China are putting off marriage, they are educated and have a career path. They are earning a higher income. They have a choice: economic independence vs. early marriage. The simple fact is that the women are in the demographic driver's seat in China, and the young women will be for years to come. Their male counterparts have not been able to save enough money yet to afford to buy a decent apartment in Beijing. Chinese women prefer men who have the potential to earn a higher income than themselves. Men are more content with married life in comparison to women, who feel additional pressure to maintain a career while taking care of their children, elderly parents or grandparents, and household chores. Similarly, women around the world, who are working full-time and managing a household, express the same frustrations while husbands can focus solely on their careers. These inequities have led to an increase in the divorce rate in China and other countries around the world. "With rapid economic growth, China has undergone substantial social, cultural, and ideological transformations over recent decades. China's divorce rate has witnessed a steady and noticeable increase in the recent two decades, with the Crude Divorce Rate (CDR) increasing by 178% and Refined Divorce Rate (RDR) increasing by 211%."[165] "The marriage rate in China has continued to decline since 2014 as a result of a decrease in population due to the implementation of the family planning policy rate in the 1970s and 1980s, said Yang Zongtao, an official with the ministry in Beijing, noting that changing concepts about marriage have also played a part."[166]

In Japan, the situation between men and women's social relationships is very bizarre and at a dangerous stage. In 2018, Netflix, with Christiane Amanpour produced a documentary entitled "Sex and Love Around the World." It explored relationships in various countries around the world. In Tokyo, Japan, there are sexless marriages, skin touching clubs, and clubs promoting the intimate needs of both men and women. When Japanese men want to interact with women, they are at a loss of how to display their affections or be intimate with a woman. It is socially acceptable for both men and women to remain single until a late age. Young people do not date. The two sexes do not interact. Men and most women are so focused on education and work that they do not acquire the necessary social skills to meet the opposite sex. "Japanese men pay exorbitant amounts of money to learn how to behave around women. During socialization lessons, they are taught how to lay their heads in the laps of women, who touch them on their face. There is no sexual touching, but they have to be taught the basics of how to feel comfortable with the opposite sex."[167] "The birth rate is so low that Japan may have a severe labor shortage in the future. This labor shortage may be overcome with automation and imported labor. What is killing the Japanese economy is the lack of working age people paying taxes into their social security system. There is no follow-up generation paying taxes to take care of the older receding generation. The majority of the Japanese population comprises of older adults.[168] This decline in population is an extreme situation in Japan where men and women have segregated themselves. They are not prepared for marriage. The population has decreased substantially without a significant number of new births. The population of Japan is set to fall from 126.5 million in 2017 to 51 million in 2115.[169]

"This is a drastic change from the history of Japan when poor women were known as "comfort women." They were drafted by the government to "sexually service" military men."[170] Japanese women are now much more sexually aroused than men. This feeling is due to the freedom from societal constraints from the past.

"Egypt treated its women better than any of the other major civilizations of the ancient world. The Egyptians believed that joy and happiness were legitimate goals of life and regarded home and family as the major source of delight."[171] Although men were considered the head of the household, women yielded considerable power by raising the children and running the household. There are no records noting marriage ceremonies, but there are divorce court documents. Once couples began living together, it was considered a legal relationship. This relationship is like the legal definition of "common law marriage" in our own culture. In Egyptian society, adultery and sexual relations with married women were forbidden. During that time, children were a gift of happiness for a family. However, there was an exceedingly high death rate among women during childbirth. Many men and women had more than one spouse during their lifetime.

Most interesting, women in ancient Egypt were equal to men in the eyes of the law about property ownership, the ability to borrow money and sign contracts, divorce proceedings, and even appear as a witness in the courts. A woman could also be chosen and rule Egypt as Pharaoh in special circumstances. The King of Egypt could have several wives, but only one woman functioned as the Queen. Monogamy seems to have been the norm for the rest of the citizens. Some men did father children with servant girls whose wives were unable to conceive children.[172]

Christiane Desroches Noblecourt was a French Egyptologist. She was the author of many books on Egyptian art and history. She played an important role in the preservation of the Nubian Temples from flooding caused by the Aswan Dam. Her research indicated "equity between men and women during ancient Egyptian times. Temples, engravings, and statues displaying powerful and intense divinities indicate that both genders were regarded as equals and that women were not subservient to men."[173] There were over one hundred noteworthy women, female specialists recorded in every domain of medicine in Ancient Egypt. Women were very well-educated and highly regarded in their various specializations. From the age of four years old, women received instruction in the fields of science and education. They studied geometry and hieroglyphics. They were permitted to practice in any branch of knowledge they chose. They attended remedial schools with men or all-female schools. For over seventy centuries, both middle-class men and women were offered the same educational opportunities without any sexism.[174]

Tragically, in the 21st century, gender equality, its role, and impact on Egyptian women has declined dramatically. "Traditional gender roles in Egypt are clearly defined. They are associated with traditional Islamic structures. The women's roles are strongly associated with the domestic household, while the men's role is outside of the house. There are strong gender disparities between men and women in Egypt about reproductive health, economic status, education, work, and overall empowerment. Women only make up 24% of the workforce."[175] Muslim men are permitted to have multiple wives. Women do not receive the same rights. "A United Nations study in 2013 showed that 99.3% of Egyptian women had experienced sexual harassment."[176] During the 2011 revolution in Egypt where there were tremendous political demonstrations and violence, thousands of women were subjected to sexual violence and rape.[177] According to the report from the Thomson Reuters Foundation, Egypt ranks as the worst country for women's rights in comparison to all of the 22 countries in the Arab states. This study included reproductive rights, economic status, rights within the family unit and society, political representation, and violence against women.[178]

While women's status has improved to some degree, women's empowerment in Egypt has faced many obstacles, including the country's political and economic conditions, its patriarchal social environment, and the efforts of religious extremists. While women have had full and equal right to vote since 1955, the strong legal basis for women's human rights in Egypt is often limited by a lack of proper implementation of procedures to ensure women's equal access to justice and the law. Egyptian women have also limited influence at the national and community levels, despite achieving leadership positions as ministers, ambassadors, media heads, MPs, and university professors. The state encourages groups that advocate for women's rights but is not as supportive of groups associated with women's rights who call for a greater participation in the political system.[179]

There is an ancient culture where women were not treated as property. In the Norse culture, the Vikings deserved a bad reputation for "raping and pillaging," but back home, they were very progressive in their treatment of women. They could own land and even earn the title similar to Earl, by which they could be the ruling authority over a settlement. The Norse culture was one of the few societies that had "shield maidens," women fighting alongside the male warriors in battle. Norse women also had the right to leave their husbands if they were abusive or well-known philanders. They were able to pursue marriage with another man without any punishment or public shaming.[180]

It is necessary to discuss the history of gender relationships between men and women: what their roles were and what was their purpose in society. Today, the question is whether women are losing their identity with their aspiration to be equal to men? Are women shedding their female attributes and becoming ineffective? A gender role is a set of societal norms dictating what types of behavior are considered desirable or appropriate for a person based on their sex. Socially constructed gender roles can lead to equal rights between genders. However, strict gender roles can also inhibit a society and discriminate against groups of citizens, causing severe disadvantages and unequal rights. From the very beginning of time, children emulate gender roles from the behavior of their parents and the sociocultural environment. However, gender roles have changed drastically throughout history. Equality and tolerance have not been maintained and practiced. Today, some cultures have even regressed so severely that their citizens are still shunned, abused, and beaten publicly, even maimed and killed. Women in the Arab world are, on average, severely at a disadvantage economically, politically, and socially. In these male-dominated societies, only their fathers, brothers, and husbands can tell them what they can and cannot do. They must always ask permission, even to leave home, and generally, with a family male escort.

In the United States, women's average salary is 20% lower than that of their male counterparts, despite working in the same field with higher education rates and sometimes even working longer hours. Some of the reasons for these disparities are social norms and attitudes. Economic pressures and structural forces also help maintain the status quo.[181] Thousands of women who have participated in the #MeToo Movement, are angry at the past and present behaviors of men and established societal norms. They demand change and may even feel that they don't need men. The answer is not the emasculation of men, but to make them more sensitive to women's emotional needs.

Women at times do not adhere to the gender role. Their husbands or partners have minimal expectations from them. These women abdicate all responsibilities. In these cases, men also must share the blame for the breakdown of the family unit.

The #MeToo Movement has also brought about a fundamental change within the judicial system, the prosecution of thousands of men who have sexually abused women in the past. Sexually abusive relationships have become publicized in the media. Lists of corporate men are readily available online. Hundreds of them have been forced to resign from their positions and apologize publicly. Their lives and reputations have been destroyed forever. Women's passive- aggressiveness is not helpful. According to psychologist Nick Duffell in the United Kingdom, "Men are very unskilled when it comes to relationships and dealing with emotions. They need to be trained better at vulnerability, better at relating, and when they do that, the power they develop will be more authentic."[182]

There seems to be a negative association with "patriarchy." In most gender-equal societies like Sweden, males are still at the top, and a lower percentage of females are in leadership positions. The idea that men in power are evil, is quite misguided. The patriarchal society built western culture, and the men worked hard to make the world a better place. There is corruption, but overall, the world of the west is doing better than anywhere else in the world. Competence is not a bad thing. Oppression is what is destructive. Some men become defensive about the idea of benefitting from patriarchy, but many feel they are suffering under it. "The main breadwinner is not a pleasant place to be. The person who is expected to use violence to defend people is not a good place to be. There are more men in prisons, more men in the army. Men are more likely to hurt other men, and it is because they are policing masculinity."[183]

Contrary to the feminist narrative, Western culture is, in fact, the least patriarchal in human history. Rather than forced to veil, females in our society can parade themselves around in as scantily clad manner of their choice. On April 4, 2018, on Inside Edition on ABC broadcasting, they reported that the romance novels were getting a new look on their covers. They were going to dress the men in shirts, jackets, and suits, instead of being shirtless with bare chests. They did not comment on how women will be depicted going forth with their publications. It seems that women do not have a problem with exposing their body parts in any situation, and they do not expect any repercussions from this behavior. Many women think that it is acceptable to dress scantily in the name of appearing sexy even when the look is not necessarily appropriate. The change in men's dress was to demonstrate respect for women. The authors of these romance novels stated that they would be changing their narratives. Bosses would no longer be taking advantage of their female employees or making sexual advances towards them in the storylines. They would treat them with respect. However, the "steamy sexual scenes" will still be described as they have always been written.

It is interesting to speculate why the fictional series "Fifty Shades of Grey" has been so popular.[184] In the books and the movies, the main female character was a virgin. She became very attracted to a man whom she had met. She agreed to be submissive sexually, as requested by this man. The storyline weaves a tale of her coming to understand and accept her sexual desires while wanting to be independent and be accepted for herself. From a psychiatric viewpoint, the author's explanations of why her lover behaved this way were insightful. During his upbringing, he had experienced various sexual encounters with an older woman. As the couple's sexual relationship continued, he was willing to change, not wanting to lose the woman he loved.

After a couple marries, the woman often tries to change her husband's behavior. She wants him to be the way she thinks he should be, rather than accept him for the way he was when they fell in love and decided to get married. When her partner does not change, she becomes depressed and remains married for the sake of the children, or gets divorced, or withdraws from all sexual activity, leaving the door open for extra-marital affairs by one or both partners.

Sheryl Sandberg writes: "Make your partner a real partner" in her book, "Lean In." She states: "In the last thirty years, women have made more progress in the workplace than in the home. According to the most recent analysis, when a husband and wife in the United States are both employed full-time, the wife performs 40% more childcare and about 30% more housework than the father. A 2009 survey found that 9% of people in dual wage marriages said that they shared housework, childcare, and breadwinning, evenly. In India, women do more than ten times as much childcare and nearly thirty times as much housework as men. While the men are taking on more household responsibilities, this increase in support is happening very slowly."[185]

Sandberg describes how women feel the need "to do it all." Some women grow up with this expectation from having watched their mothers take full responsibility for the household and the children. They feel that they should cook, clean, do the laundry, perform the majority of childcare, take care of the family members when they are ill, and even take care of elderly parents, and the list goes on. Regarding their work performance, they never want to be seen as slacking off in comparison to their male peers.[186]

When I was working, I always felt the need to ensure "my i's were dotted, and t's crossed" as Chief of Staff at the hospital. I did not want any of my male colleagues to find any reason to criticize me for not meeting the standards that I was imposing upon them. Some of the staff did see me as being hard on them while supervising them. Simply, I expected them to do their best. The health of our patients and their well-being were at stake. Some personnel did not work as hard for other male physicians, but I required my staff and myself to be at the top of our game.

It is interesting to question whether most women are programmed from an early age to model their behaviors after their mothers' nurturing versus being genetically programmed to behave in a more caring way through the natural formation of their DNA, which can dictate to a certain extent whether you will be a scientist, engineer, or an individual with artistic talent, etc. These traits may come directly from your family members and ancestors. Some women possess a motherly instinct, but not all women do. It is unclear whether the behaviors we display as adults are psychologically embedded in our brains from a young age. The experiences from our childhood dictate our actions throughout life. Children emulate learnt behaviors from parents, both good and bad.

It is not surprising that women are more depressed than men and feel burnt out from their daily activities. Their housework is never appreciated as much as their work in the office where they earn a salary. As a psychiatrist, I often used the analogy of the "empty bucket syndrome" for women in distress. When women continue to take care of everyone else and everything in the household, in addition to working, their bucket quickly empties. No one is looking after them, trying to lighten their responsibilities. They do not have the time or energy each day to fill their own bucket. They become overwhelmed and depressed. The recommendation for women is to find a partner in life who is willing to be a true partner in helping out with all of the household responsibilities: mundane housework, childcare, cooking, grocery shopping, laundry, care of aging parents, and other chores. Partners need to be responsible for each other and realize that things are not always equal 50-50. Sometimes the men will have to pick up the slack and do 90% of the household and child-rearing chores. Other times, the roles may be reversed when the women will have to carry the burden of the household and childrearing.

When looking for a life partner, Sheryl Sandberg's advice to women is "to date all of them: the bad boys, the good boys, the commitment-phobic boys, the crazy boys, but do not marry them. The things that make the bad boys sexy do not make them good husbands. When it comes time to settle down with a partner, find someone who wants to be an equal partner. Look for someone who thinks women should be smart, opinionated, and ambitious, and someone who values fairness and wants to contribute his share of responsibilities in the home. These men are rare, but they do exist."[187]

I would highly recommend one other requirement when looking for a life partner. Find someone who makes you laugh and enjoys laughing often. Laughter will decrease conflicts. It is easier to get over being angry when you can tease each other and laugh together. Men do not have to feel ashamed if they must help out more in the household. They can still have their "macho" image and are most definitely not "mama's boys" for helping to run a smooth household where all the family members are happy and working together. If men are confident in their male roles, nothing is belittling about doing dishes or laundry or taking a sick day to take care of an ill child or parent.

Sandberg also advises that women do not need to be perfect at everything. "Done is better than perfect."[188] Set priorities. Men and women need to be strong enough to let go of things that make them anxious and unhappy. While working full-time, I needed to make sure that my house was clean, neat, and dusted, especially when expecting company. Eventually, I recognized that our friends were coming over to spend time with us rather than review the condition of our home. I also became anxious when preparing a meal for our guests. I wanted it to be perfect. Now I enjoy trying new recipes and believe in my culinary skills. I know that the meal will be "edible." With age and experience comes confidence.

The Yin and the Yang

The ancient yin-yang symbol, sometimes called ying-yang, is a Chinese symbol that represents balance. The name "yin-yang" can be translated from Chinese into English as "dark and light." They are two opposite forces that are represented in the symbol pictured in black and white. It conveys the idea of fundamental unity within all of creation, based on a dynamic interplay between complementary opposites.

Yin – "Women" are described as soft, weak, dark, receptive, and passive, (black)

Yang – "Men" are described as hard, dominating, bright, expansive, and assertive.[189] (white)

Men and women are supposed to complement each other but do not have to be necessarily equal. Women have been taught to be obedient, subservient to their fathers and then to their husbands. Around the world, gender roles are still predetermined from years ago in the ancient Asian cultures and to some extent, this is expected of women from all cultures. They have been raised to be submissive no matter what their level of education. It is important to examine how to change those cultural expectations without causing a breakdown in relationships between men and women. Presently, the source of conflict on both sides is due to gender roles not being clearly defined as they used to be in the past.

Men were stronger, bigger, and usually taller than women. They were food gathers and protectors against predators. Women were smaller in stature and weaker than men. They stayed at home and prepared the meals, bore children, and took care of them. The roles were clearly defined. Men and women understood their positions in society.

Before the Civil War, women stayed home to take care of their children and performed household chores while men were the breadwinners. Post-Civil War, this ideology began to shift as women began to enter the workforce. Women developed a newfound sense of freedom. Today in the 21st century, we not only have women working, but many of them have chosen life-long careers. It is interesting to explore how they now fit into the family unit. In the United States, the U.S. Department of Labor established "The Women's Bureau" on June 5, 1920. A law was passed to "formulate standards and policies to promote the welfare of wage-earning women, improve their working conditions, increase their efficiency, and advance their opportunities for profitable employment."[190] The Bureau also received the authority to report and investigate all matters relating to women throughout industry. One hundred years later, as "The Women's Bureau" celebrates its centennial, women still struggle to receive equal pay and opportunities.

During World War II, thousands of women participated in the labor market while so many men were serving in the military. Women had to take jobs to support the war effort and to support their families while their husbands and fathers were serving overseas. Also, 350,000 American women joined the military. They worked as nurses, truck drivers, airplane technicians, and office workers, even airplane pilots. Over 1,100 women were trained and flew every type of military aircraft, including B-26 and B-29 bombers. They flew military flights from factories to military bases and departure points throughout the country. After the planes were repaired, they tested them. They were members of the WASP, an organization founded and based on the efforts of two interesting female aviators, Jacky Cochran and Nancy Love. All these outstanding, brave women assisted the military efforts of the United States. Sadly, the organization was disbanded after two years.[191]

In the 1950s, the percentage of American women in the workforce rose to 34%. "These increases were due to businesses needing clerical workers and new technologies, along with a tremendous number of women attending high school in the 20th century. It is important to note that the women's participation within the labor force was negatively affected as their husbands' income rose. The higher the income, the less she would have to work outside the home."[192] Shortly, that behavior would change as more and more young women in the 1960s and 70s began to attend college and obtain a degree. However, with the feminist movement of the 1960s, women began to enter the workforce in great numbers. "At this time, the introduction of birth control and the contraceptive pill in the United States gave women more control over childbearing. The pill had the effects of increasing female work participation and narrowing gender pay inequality."[193] "In 1999, there was the highest number of women working outside of the home. Over 60.3% of women over the age of sixteen were employed."[194] But in the early 2000s, that rise came to a halt. The Great Recession arrived in 2007. "Since that time, there has been a decline, a small decrease to 57% in the number of women working in America."[195]

In 2020, there is still the major issue of how women can obtain equality in the workplace. Career-minded women, especially with professional degrees, who choose not to have children and do not have the responsibility of taking care of aging parents, will certainly fare better in the job marketplace. To give women equal parity, the following conditions should be instituted in American society:

1. Make childcare affordable and accessible.
2. Institute explicit sexual harassment policies with transparency in the workplace. (Note: The following three recommendations are brought up frequently without taking into consideration how they affect the company, and why they are not feasible.)
3. Pay women for maternity and family sick leave.
4. Enforce the same expectations of both men and women in the workplace.
5. Equalize wages and salaries for the same position held by men and women.

Some of the reasons behind the inequality may be understood by the following examples.

If a man and a woman both join a company on the same day, it is somehow expected that 20 years later, all things being equal, that they will rise to the same position at an equitable salary level. Yet, at the same time, people want the woman to be able to leave for many months (or in California, for two years) for maternity leave. During those two years, she contributes nothing to the company, and the company is forced to hire additional temporary workers. The concept is appealing but it does not work from a company perspective.

Women's health issues and family responsibilities are considerable when relating to employment. All companies tend to face substantial losses in revenues due to employees going on maternity leave or taking care of sick family members. Even large companies do not have available excess workers to take on the responsibilities of an individual on a leave of absence. During the pregnancies, there are a considerable number of healthcare visits to the doctor's office. Sometimes, complications occur with pregnancy, and women are required to stay home and seek bed rest. Coworkers are needed to assist with the increased workload when pregnant coworkers miss work. They could feel resentment towards the homebound staff member.

As an employer with two candidates, a male and a female with the same professional resume, education, and experience, applying for a position, this situation presents a challenge. Depending upon the ages of both candidates, the employer may choose the male over the female. It is a quiet type of a sex discrimination. Employers are not allowed to ask age-related questions, but your date of birth appears on many employment applications. They are also not permitted to ask if you have children or are responsible for elderly parents. In many respects, as a woman, employment and advancement opportunities are not easily obtained.

Sheryl Sandberg in her book, *Lean In* has advocated that employers should ask prospective employees about their plans regarding marriage, children, child, and eldercare.[196] Employers do not necessarily see these lifestyle options as negative when they find the right candidate for the position. Provisions and plans can be made to accommodate the employee. Sandberg suggests that families, both the husband and the wife, may need to pay for child or elder care expenses. These costs must be considered as an investment in the woman's career if she genuinely wants to move up the corporate ladder and is dedicated to her work. Many times, the cost of childcare equals a woman's salary. Tough financial decisions must be made within the family. Sometimes, more substantial companies may absorb these additional costs when hiring a high-level employee. Today, many companies are also offering paternal leave for new fathers in the workplace, but the amount of time is nowhere near what is offered for maternity leave. "However, paid paternity leave is rare in the United States. American men who have access to paid leave do not always take what is available to them, in part because they are getting messages, whether implicit or explicit, that they will be punished for taking that time away from work. While a far greater number of American women take maternity leave, just under half, get paid time off, and they may feel pressure to do some work while they are off."[197]

Although Sandberg recommended that employers should speak to their prospective employees about marriage and family, it is prohibited by law. "The U.S. Equal Employment Opportunity Commission (EEOC) is responsible for enforcing federal laws that make it illegal to discriminate against a job applicant or an employee because of a person's race, color, religion, sex (including pregnancy, gender identity, and sexual orientation), national origin, age (40 or older), disability or genetic information. In addition, the laws apply to all types of work situations, including hiring, firing, promotions, harassment, training, wages, and benefits."[198]

For the most part, women are mainly responsible for their children when they are sick, off from school, or on vacation. They are required to take days off from work or hire a babysitter. At times, they are obligated to stay home because they were unable to find a caregiver for their children. Hopefully, both parents can share the childcare responsibilities when they are working full-time. Working families also face additional challenges when caring for elderly or sick relatives. The baby boomer generation and other adults are taking time off from work to take parents to doctors' appointments, the grocery store, and perform other weekly errands. Many parents are no longer able to drive due to illnesses or disabilities. Again, often women become the primary caregivers for their parents and relatives.

Today, many women have joined the military, and as recruits and inducted soldiers, they are required to travel and serve during their deployment. Often, they are sent thousands of miles away from home for extended periods away from their families. If women have young children, they can apply for a voluntary discharge, which ends their military careers. All branches of the military provide women with six weeks of maternity leave. "In January 2019, the Army doubled the amount of parental leave for fathers and other secondary caregivers of newborn infants from ten to twenty-one days."[199]

Service in the military has other challenges for women. Females can train as hard as men, but most of them are not as strong as men because of the different physical morphologies of the two sexes. Females cannot carry some of the weapons required for specific missions. The "dynamic" of the team changes when females are included with male members on military operations. Male members may feel more protective of female members of the squad. This gender sensitivity could affect the outcome of a military mission.

The #MeToo Movement has given rise to another significant legal issue that needs to be addressed when hiring women in the workplace. Should companies think about segregating men and women in the work environment for fear of future sexual harassment accusations or lawsuits? Do managers have to worry about inappropriate male or female behavior in the office setting? What kind of policies need to be firmly established in order to avoid legal harassment suits? Employers must be aware of hiring the most professional individuals to avoid any future consequences of inappropriate sexual behavior. Sensitivity training is essential for all staff, so casual comments are not misinterpreted between men and women. Men often joke amongst themselves, and now they have to pay attention if there are women nearby. Recently, even Joe Biden, a candidate for the Presidential election of 2020, has been accused of whispering in women's ears and touching their hair.[200] Tara Reade, a former Biden staffer, filed a criminal complaint with the Washington, DC, police on April 9, 2020 accusing the former vice president of sexually assaulting her in 1993. A campaign spokesperson put out a statement "Women have a right to tell their story, and reporters have an obligation to rigorously vet those claims. We encourage them to do so because these accusations are false."

Sheryl Sandberg reported that in her late husband's company, a survey was performed and reported that senior executive men were three and half times more likely to hesitate to take a junior female staff member to dinner than a junior male staff employee. And they were five times more hesitant to travel with a junior female staff member than a male employee. Sandberg feels that women deserve the same access and mentorship that men receive.[201] However, in this climate of men facing any form of sexual harassment with or without proof or justification, male corporate executives are most cautious. Their careers can easily be destroyed in this climate of warranted and unwarranted litigation. The #MeToo Movement has affected the hiring practices of many corporations across the nation.

In China, the government has expended outstanding economic resources to educate young women and provide them with equal opportunities in the job marketplace. Recently, government officials fear that young males in society have become too submissive to females. Chinese schools and daycare centers are designing playtime activities to increase the masculinity traits in young boys. It is believed that parents have over-protected these young boys. They have become physically and emotionally weak due to their parents' over-indulgent behaviors and fear of losing their only child. Boys have lost their natural, adventurous spirit. They are now being trained to be strong, brave, and behave more aggressively toward their female counterparts.[202]

Many young Chinese women believe in premarital sex and feel that it will lead to a marriage proposal. Chinese men prefer to marry a young woman who is a virgin. Dating is taken very seriously. If a woman is still single at 27 years old, she is in "the left-over category." She is stigmatized as "sheng nu."[203] These women are pressured from their families to marry, stemming from the widespread belief that regardless of education or professional achievement, a woman is "nothing until she is married."

Single women in India also face discrimination if they are not married by the age of 25 years old. If a young Indian woman is pursuing a career or studying in college, it is permissible for her to remain single. Personally, as an Indian woman, I felt the pressure to be married. All my cousins were married in their early twenties, but my parents expected me to finish medical school before considering marriage. I was twenty-five years old at the time and had been dating my boyfriend for nine years. His parents were expecting him to have an arranged marriage. I was terrified that if I did not marry him, I would be subjected to an arranged marriage after graduating from medical school.

Today, the question is: what is affecting the dynamics of the relationships between men and women?

Men report that in their minds, they are younger than their chronological age. They can impregnate a woman until a late age, if they are able to have sex or through a sperm bank. Genetically, they may have difficulty accepting their real age. Men have minimal complaints about older men marrying younger women for love or to have trophy wives. Most of these young wives do not need to work. They may not be involved in performing housework or raising children. In fact, often older men with young wives are thought to be wealthy.

Interestingly, older women with handsome, young men as partners are not thought of in the same way. People may assume that she must be his mother. In general, older women do not take care of themselves physically. They do not exercise and stay fit. Instead, they become complacent, overweight, tired-looking, and unhealthy. Medically, it is an interesting fact that women outlive men by several years. There is a disproportionate number of older women to older men.

When women start thinking that they do not need men, it is a serious problem in society. Women have become more self-reliant. They can become pregnant, bear children, and raise families without a man around, but at what expense? Couples are still getting married. However, around the globe in most countries, the age for getting married has increased dramatically. Many young people are choosing to never get married. Americans still marry more often than individuals from other Western nations, but also obtain more divorces than any other country.[204] While marriage is often seen as an essential step to a successful life, the Pew Research Center reports that only about 50% of Americans over the age of eighteen are married. This percentage of married individuals has decreased from 72% of Americans in 1960. On average, people are getting married much later in life. In the United States, the median age for a first marriage rose to an all-time high in 2018: age 30 for men and 28 for women. While most Americans expect to marry eventually, 14% of adults who have never married, report that they do not plan to marry at all. And another 28% report that they are not sure whether marriage is for them.[205]

Couples are choosing to live together and have children, but do not feel the need to get married. Is this a custom perpetrated by religion? Couples are committing to a relationship without having to bring the government's involvement in their personal life. The cost of weddings has become outrageous. In the past, a wedding celebration was held in one's family home with family and close friends bringing food to share. Now, the guest list, sometimes in the hundreds, the cost of a wedding dress only worn once, and meals for all the guests can very easily add up to thousands of dollars. I have experienced parents who have gone through their savings or taken out loans, so their daughters could have "the perfect wedding day." Unfortunately, so often, this turns out to be a waste of money with the high divorce rate in the United States. And to add insult to injury, it may cost thousands of dollars to get out of a marriage with a divorce lawyer. That money could have been spent on a down payment for a house or college loan debt.

Many of the millennials are not getting married until later in life. Career women are getting married but having children later in life. Delays in marriage and childbirth are affecting the genetic pool and skewing the population of the next generation. Older couples are having fewer children. Many of them are unable to conceive when they finally decide to become pregnant. These repercussions are already evident in the societies of Europe, Japan, and China, and to some extent, the United States. Some individuals in the United States continue to have multiple children since they are ensured to receive additional financial aid on welfare, and refuse to be responsible, and use birth control. Other families, due to religious beliefs, also do not use contraception. Working parents may realize early on in their marriage or cohabitation that raising children is very costly, and then limit the number of children they will have to only one or two.

In 2005, a third of single Japanese people, ages 18 to 34, were virgins. In 2015, the percentage had increased to 43%, and more adults reported that they had no intention of getting married. The dichotomy is that Japan is the world's top producer and consumer of porn, and the originator of new porn genres.[206] Originally, low employment prospects in Japan drove many men to solitary sexual pursuits, but the culture has since moved to accommodate and even encourage those activities. Roland Kelts, a Japanese American writer, explains that "this generation finds the unexpected demands of real-world relationships with women less enticing than the lure of the virtual libido."[207]

As a society, we must ask ourselves how men will react over time if we continue to de- masculinize them. Men and women do enjoy being together. They enjoy intimacy. Will men shy away from relationships and commitments to a partner if they will be continually criticized? Most women enjoy receiving compliments from men, even from strangers. Women also enjoy flirting with men. Women will even admit that their sole purpose for flirting was to encourage a man, to perform a task that needed to get done. Both men and women go to bars to meet and pick-up partners, even for a night. Women even use men to get pregnant without the man's consent. Women have become less sexually repressed, and their expectations to hook-up casually are just as strong as men's desires.

"Everyone is trying to find the right person,
but nobody is trying to be the right person."[208]
Prince Ea

Men also deserve to be spoiled. They also need to be told that they are handsome. Their efforts need to be appreciated. They should also be made to feel secure. If he treats you like a "queen," treat him like a "king." A man by his nature is solid, loving, kind, and protective. He is not threatened by his own femininity or the external feminine. He knows how to make a woman feel valued. Men are perceived to have power, yet most of the men feel powerless about their own lives, emotions, and personal connections. It is a start for men to acknowledge these feelings and work on these issues.

Judith Newman published an article in the New York Times about the book *Lean In* five years later. Several women were interviewed to understand if the information in the book affected them in any way and to find out if it had been helpful to them to climb the corporate ladder. One of the women, Alix Lawson, twenty-seven years old, a senior program associate for Freedom House, a non-governmental organization in Washington, appreciated that Sandberg presented women without taking on the role of the victim. She perceived it as a lesson in being a strong woman, being able to accomplish things without sacrificing one's professionalism. In her personal life, she mentioned that she had an argument with her grandmother, who told her that "a real man always pays." When Lawson was out on a date, she felt more comfortable splitting the tab. She did not want to feel that she "owed something." She likes Sandberg's idea of "full- sharing."[209]

In all honesty, one wonders how many women share or pick up the tab, or just expect the man to pay when going out on a date. I have never understood why men have to bear this burden. If two or more friends are going out to have a good time and both are earning money, why does the man have to pay on most occasions? I have always either paid or reciprocated the next time, except when the person taking me out, had insisted that this was their treat. In this case, women are happy to accept men's chivalry without any questions.

> *"Don't let the history of gender define what happens in the future, and don't let it define your future."*[210]
>
> *Author Unknown*

When deciphering the gender differences, males are more vocal, and sometimes even vulgar in their comments. It does not mean that they are weak or pathetic. Most of them are not trying to take advantage of women because they are in an authoritative position. However, both sexes, men and women in authoritative positions have been known to abuse their authority over their subordinates. Men may worry that they will be ridiculed or seen as weak if they complain. There is no excuse for any individual, whether male or female, to behave in this manner. Sexual harassment, emotional, and physical abuse have no place in any environment. Women may feel empowered by the #MeToo Movement, but we need to consider the bigger picture, and the anger that is being expressed. All the negativity against men is not going to advance women's role in society. Women's alienation of men will lead to the destruction of good working relationships between men and women. Men will not want to marry women who consider men to be predators and weak individuals who have difficulty controlling their sexual urges.

The differences between men and women have been addressed for many years. Everyone has heard of the book *Men are from Mars, and Women are from Venus*. There is an age-old answer about what men understand about women: "nothing!" Women think they know men, but many women do not comprehend their needs or ways of thinking. Women are obsessed about having men conform to their thought processes in a relationship, much to their detriment.

Men are viewed as more sexual, but surely it takes both men and women to get involved sexually." Why do women need to dress scantily? Shorts have gotten shorter and tighter. Their breasts are exposed or pushed up. Many women's dresses barely cover their "private parts." Just notice the gowns that actresses wear at the Oscars or entertainers who are performing at concerts. Even young girls and teenagers wear next to nothing at the beach. It is a personal choice of how individuals dress and how comfortable they are at exposing their bodies. Even other women are offended when they see women dressed scantily and inappropriately in social situations. Everyone is indeed entitled to dress in whatever manner they choose. However, it is respectful to others when we all observe the rules of society. Many women go to the gym clad in a sports bra and leggings. Men are not allowed to wear cut-off tee shirts and expose their midriffs. It seems that the staff at gyms have different standards for men and women. Men's brains are programmed to react differently as compared to women's minds. We cannot expect men to be the only ones making changes in their behavior. Women, too, must demonstrate restraint in their habits of dressing if they want to be respected.

"You can't change other people. You can only change yourself."[211]

Lorraine Bracco

Roles of Men and Women in the Workplace

In April 2018, an article was published in the newsletter "Imprimis," a publication of Hillsdale College. It reportedly has 3.7 million monthly readers, and their website lists 5.4 million subscribers. The article was entitled "The Negative Impact of the #MeToo Movement." Heather MacDonald of the Manhattan Institute wrote it. She stated that our nation is about to be transformed due to the #MeToo Movement. "If the only consequence were to stop sexual predation, that would be good. However, the effects of the movement are going to be sweeping and destructive. Corporations are scrambling to review their gender and race quotas, on the theory that all disparities in employment and institutional representations are due to harassment and bias. The decision making may be influenced negatively, and the best candidates for the job, regardless of gender or race, could be passed over in the drive for gender parity."[212]

A 2007 survey of the Harvard Business School alumni found that full-time employment was at 81% for young women who graduated in the early 2000s and only at 49% for women who graduated in the early 1990s. In comparison, the men's full-time employment rate never fell below 91%. Yale alumni who had reached their forties by the year 2000, only 56% of women remained in the workforce compared to 90% of the men. This exodus of highly educated women is a major contributor to the leadership gap. When women are married to men with greater economic resources, they tend to leave the workforce for several reasons. When professional men work fifty or more hours per week, wives with children are 44% more likely to quit their jobs.[213] Sheryl Sandberg stated "it is easy for women to drop out of the workforce because they feel that they bear the primary responsibility for raising the children. Men, on the other hand, feel that they bear the primary responsibility of supporting their families financially, hence making it harder for them to drop out of the workforce. Their self-worth is tied mainly to their professional success, and they frequently believe they have no choice in the matter."[214]

Sunny Bates, chief executive of Sunny Bates Associates, a management consulting company, reported that Sheryl Sandberg was honest and made women question not just what is wrong with the corporate structure but forced them to ask several questions. "How are you holding yourself back? When there is a problem, what is your role in this situation?"[215] She feels that we will all have to grow through being uncomfortable, asking difficult questions, and looking at ourselves to make changes. Ms. Bates admitted that she had put her husband at the center of everything, and it was a terrible marriage. Her career took off when she got a divorce.

This same result is often real for men who are stuck in bad marriages. Once they leave an unhappy marriage, they become more successful in business. They have less stress in their personal lives. Wives often spend way beyond the family budget. Men must continue to work long hours to support their wives' bad financial habits. In my psychiatric practice, several men came into therapy because they were frustrated and needed to learn to set financial limits for their wives and teach them how to budget. If husbands and wives do not learn how to work on family finances together, there will be significant financial and emotional problems in the marriage. Men can also cause financial difficulties with the family budget by overspending on "boy toys." They feel entitled because they are bringing home the paychecks.

Gender, diversity, and inclusion were the dominant themes at the 2018 World Economic Forum in Davos, Switzerland. It was chaired exclusively by women. U.S. banks and financial institutions are facing pressure from shareholder groups to release data on the number and compensation of females and minorities in their upper ranks. People have become intolerant to looking at things from a different perspective. Immediate punishment is doled out on anyone in business who has shown the courage to criticize this war on merit.[216] In August 2017, Google fired computer engineer James Damore for writing a memo suggesting that the lack of 50-50 gender proportionality at Google and other tech companies may not be due to bias, but rather to different preferences on the part of males and females.[217]

Ridiculous statements as expressed by New York Senator Kirsten Gillibrand "the New York Fed has never been led by a woman or a person of color, and that needs to change,"[218] is a cry from the diversocrats. They are determined to fill the upper-rank positions with women or people of color, regardless of who is the most qualified person for the job. It is important to state that perhaps in the past, women and people of color were overlooked, and preference was given to white males. We must not get carried away in the opposite direction. We must ask ourselves if "white men" are now in jeopardy when individuals insist that the upper ranks of professional positions must be filled only with women and people of color to meet company quotas. The pendulum always swings from one extreme to the other, and unfortunately not without major repercussions. It is dangerous to blindly follow leaders of this movement without considering all the consequences going forward.

The 30% club first launched in the United Kingdom in 2010 had an inspirational goal of 30% women on FTSE-100 boards by the end of 2015. It has moved from 12.5% women directors in 2010 to 20.8% as of March 2014, with the 30% club as a driving force behind the change. Club supporters in the United Kingdom have focused on creating better gender balance by targeting talent management practices, executive search firms, shareholders, schools, and universities.[219] Many countries in Europe have regulated the makeup of boards requiring a certain percentage of women. This may or may not be a good thing depending if there are sufficient qualified women willing to serve on boards, or if they are just staffing them with whomever they can find to meet the law.[220]

Peter Grauer, Chairman of Bloomberg L.P., was selected to serve as founding United States Chairperson in 2014. Gender imbalance at senior levels is a global phenomenon, and they want to develop a pipeline of female talent in U.S. organizations. "This is a business issue as much as it is a diversity issue. Businesses do better when they avoid 'group think,' and better gender balance is a key factor in business success. We have a lot more work to do in the U.S. to improve female representation, and senior business leaders have to drive that change,"[221] Grauer stated. Women taking on higher administrative roles have helped to highlight the problems of leadership and sexual harassment or assault from powerful males in the United States and abroad.

Corporations are forced to spend sometimes unnecessary and expensive resources to collect all this data, putting policies in place and providing sensitivity training for men and women, so they can work together. The bottom line should be the best person is hired for the job; men are better at some tasks than women; women are better at some tasks than men, and there will always be sexual banter between men and women.

Men need to be more sensitive and avoid outrageous sexist comments and actions towards women in the workplace. Women also need to be mindful of the impact of talking about private issues in front of male co-workers. Women have been known to make crude remarks in mixed company and think nothing of how males react to these comments. In many situations, there are double standards. Some women do not want to hear what men have to say and become easily offended. Other women have minimal reservations about things that women and men may discuss socially without any concerns. People need to be aware of what to say, where to say it, and who is around before saying things that may be construed as inappropriate. Women and men must show mutual respect.

Women should not be "overly sensitive" to sexual remarks but learn to speak up when they are made to feel uncomfortable without demanding repercussions when the conversations were meant to be casual. They must have the courage to learn to approach the individuals who have offended them and try to resolve the issues between them. They do not always need to involve the management staff. Harassment policies must be established and enforced in the workforce. Emotions drive the thought processes of both men and women and influence the decisions they make. They must be willing to recognize their feelings and discuss them openly for better cooperation and work productivity.

Another issue discussed in *Lean In* was understanding that there is "my point of view," which is "my truth." And there is someone else's point of view that is "their truth." Rarely is their "one absolute truth." When we recognize that we can only see things from our perspective, we will be able to share our views in a non-threatening way with others.

It has been suggested that women have a difficult time asking for pay raises or pointing out to their superiors their positive contributions to their department or company, without fearing repercussions. However, it should be noted that many men also have the same fears. Both men and women may have contributed tremendously, especially in start-up companies where they have invented or improved technology. In the end, their company takes all the credit, and they do not compensate the workers appropriately for their efforts.

Some individuals feel that there is an issue with female bosses viewed in a negative light. They are being too hard on employees. Sheryl Sandberg explains that this may be because of one's perception of females. They are "supposed to be gentle, nice, and motherly." However, bosses must be assertive and demanding at times, especially when companies are experiencing significant difficulties. Calling your female boss "crazy" or "hysterical" has sexist undertones, because these words have a long, problematic history. In the past, especially in

19th century Europe, women who had anxiety or who were troublemakers, were often diagnosed as being 'hysterical.' The word 'hysterical' comes from the Greek word hystera, meaning uterus, signifying that the so-called disease was specific to women.[222]

Some male bosses are also seen in a negative light, but men get away with being ruthless as "fathers in the family are usually the disciplinarians."[223] A supervisor expects a certain amount of work, production, appropriate and ethical behavior, and his job is to monitor all employees. Management and employee issues must be addressed, and the work environment improved. It is essential to remember that bosses in your workplace are not your friends. Their jobs are to supervise employees and accomplish the required work for corporate success and enhanced profitability. Both men and women need to learn to work with supervisors of the opposite sex and not make it a male/female issue.

Sexual Behaviors and Why They Bond Men and Women

In most cultures, the past generation of men and women never openly showed affection towards each other. How many of us remember parents touching each other, holding hands, or kissing in front of their children? Sex was a taboo subject, and even now, parents are reluctant to educate or talk to their children about sex or sexually charged topics. In the age of #MeToo Movement and the wake of the Brett Kavanaugh hearings, parents across the country have been trying to understand how to raise their teenage boys to understand the word "consent."[224] How can mothers and fathers prevent their teenage sons from being accused of sexual assault someday? Teaching sex education and discussing sexual consent to teenagers is still a relatively new concept. In previous decades, conversations about "the birds and the bees" focused on sexual abstinence, or at most, use of protection during sexual intercourse. In recent years, consent has gradually made its way into school curricula for sex education, but the programs are still rare.

Only 24 states and the District of Columbia require sex education in public schools. Fewer than a dozen states mention the terms "healthy relationships, sexual assault, or consent," in their sex education programs, according to a report in May 2020 by the Liberal Center for American Progress. Three of those states, Maryland, Rhode Island, and Missouri passed legislation this year mandating consent education, propelled by the #MeToo Movement. It is not clear how many private schools are teaching sex education in their schools. Some students in Catholic schools state they learned about sex in religion classes.

With the entertainment industry portraying all types of sexual activity on cable television or in the movies, children are much more educated about sexual activity. In the past, boys learned about sex by looking through their father's pornographic magazines, usually found under their parents' bed. Even today, Asian cultures have difficulty displaying any show of affection in public. The Indian Bollywood movies have chosen to follow the Hollywood lead. Now Indian actors and actresses kiss on screen, show some nudity in bed, and display sexual behavior to some extent. Recently, there was a Bollywood movie preview about four female friends and a wedding. They were trying to find a word for the big "O" in the Indian language. They could only come up with the expression "intense pleasure." In the past, there were only scenes in movies where couples were hugging on the screen, and everything else was left to the imagination. Couples ran around in the gardens, chasing each other, and somehow got pregnant.

Humans are sexual beings. Human DNA closely matches the DNA of primates. We have desires and needs that are fulfilled in many ways. Sexual satisfaction can be achieved in a variety of ways, even as we age. Our sexuality remains with us. Healthy, safe sex is an appropriate and vital part of our lives. It is also an activity that is required to help women conceive due to changes that occur in the body with regular sex. Other than artificial insemination, the sexual act must be performed to be able to procreate. Emotional connection thrives on sexual intimacy. The idea of coming together as a couple to give one another joy through touch and play provides us with that sense of emotional well-being we need as humans. People with strong social interactions and emotional connections live longer lives. Sexual activity helps an individual stay calm and relaxed. The body does not react as strongly to stress. Numerous examples exist of women made available to men during times of war and in the military to help soldiers deal with stress. Women can still be found around army bases "to service" the young men to help them deal with their fears and frustrations so far away from home. These women also provide companionship, and perhaps, they hope to find a husband.

Brothels are a lucrative business, and even now, prostitutes are available in all corners of the world for men's pleasure. Masturbation may help, to some extent, but physical interaction is needed between human beings to feel the relief they are seeking. Rape occurs when men become so frustrated, and in their distorted way of thinking, they justify forcing themselves onto women. Rape cases are unheard of or underreported in communities where sexual activity is more open and not seen as a taboo subject. The definition of rape varies between countries, so accurate statistics are difficult to calculate.

There is a new phenomenon called the "swipe culture" where couples hook up for a quick encounter, and then move onto the next one another day. There used to be one-night stands; now, there are half-nightstands. The younger generation would rather have sex, leave, and go to sleep in their own bed. This way, they can wake up in the morning, check their text messages and emails, get dressed in their own home, and get to work after following their morning routine. It is less awkward than having to say goodbye just before having to go to work. The millennials can compartmentalize sex and love. Sex is merely an activity. Love is intimate and has deeper meaning. Half-nightstands are often a detriment to meaningful human connection, especially if all you want to do is "have sex." You may feel satisfied physically, but if sex is used to cultivate an emotional relationship, some individuals may feel even more lonely after the hook-up. Half-nightstands can become more complicated if feelings are involved, and if the individuals are emotionally needy.

Kate Julian asked the question, "Why are young people having so little sex?"[225] Despite the easing of taboos, Americans are amid a sex recession. The consensus is that sex between unmarried adults is not at all wrong. New cases of HIV are at an all-time low. Most women have access to free birth control and the morning-after pill without a prescription.

Surprisingly, young people are not hooking up more often.[226] Some blame the digital life with interfering with their sex life, even if they are in relationships. When young and older adults are focused on watching television, marathon binge-watching of their favorite shows, streaming videos, scrolling through their phones, and playing video games, their primal hunger for sex takes a back seat. Who would have guessed that messing around online would be more satisfying than having sex or being intimate?

Millennials are focusing on work, making money, securing financial stability before looking for intimacy and relationships. In the past generation, many young adults moved out of the house by the age of eighteen. Now a record number of Millennials are living at home for a longer time before they can afford to move out on their own. This situation may have put a damper on their sexual encounters. About 60% of adults under the age of thirty-five now live without a spouse or partner.[227] One in three individuals within this age range live with their parents. Dating websites like Grindr or Tinder, help single or married people hook-up to find people with similar interests for a quick get-together or offer the prospect of casual sex within the hour. The time of instant gratification is here!

A survey by the Centers for Disease Control and Prevention's Youth Risk Behavior Surveillance System finds that from 1991 to 2017, the percentage of high school students who had intercourse dropped from 54% to 40%.[228] It was a relief for parents and educators to find out that more teens were waiting to have sex. However, some analysts perceive this delay as the first indication of a broader withdrawal from physical intimacy that extends into adulthood.

Research performed by Jean Twenge, a psychology professor at San Diego State University published in her book *iGen*, that today's young adults are on track to have fewer sex partners than members of the two preceding generations.[229] Individuals in their twenties are two and a half times as likely to be abstinent in comparison to Generation Xers at their age. 15% of them have reported that they have not had sex since they have become adults. Socialization among teenagers like dating had also decreased, in addition to other activities associated with entering adulthood, like drinking alcohol, working for a salary, going out without one's parents, and obtaining a driver's license.[230] These behavioral shifts coincide with an increase in parent's anxiety about their children's educational and economic prospects. This anxiety, especially among affluent and educated parents, has led to significant changes as to what is expected of teenagers. A young man summed up his daily life. "It is hard to work on sexual relationships when baseball practice starts at 6:30 am, classes begin at 8:15 am, drama club at 4:15 pm, working at the soup kitchen at 6 pm, and I have to finish writing a screenplay." Self- improvement and focus are the main goals of teenagers today, not relationships. The pressure from parents and other authority figures, including teachers and coaches, is overwhelming. These societal influences on young people continue through college.

Why should this lack of relationships and social connections concern society? The retreat from sexual activity is not exclusively an American phenomenon. Countries that also track their citizen's sex lives are also reporting similar declines in socialization among teenagers. In the Netherlands, this news has caused some concern. Sociologists, child psychologists, and psychiatrists feel that when teenagers skip this phase of development of sexual intimacy of flirting and kissing, and dealing with heartbreak and disappointment, they may be unprepared for the many challenges of adult life.

The divorce rate is decreasing because couples are getting married at a later age. Individuals are marrying partners who will make a good father and mother for their children and provide financial stability. People are not marrying men and women who simply want to have an affair. Casual sex might help your well-being and happiness if it is consensual and safe.

However, do not pursue this activity if you do not enjoy casual encounters. It is time to review the stigma of sex, according to people's needs. Just because you are getting older does not mean that you cannot continue to enjoy sex. There are many benefits to being sexually active.[231]

1. Sex eases stress. Being close to a partner can help decrease anxiety. Also, arousal and orgasm release the hormone oxytocin (the cuddle hormone) and decrease cortisol (the stress hormone), shutting down areas of the brain linked to fear, anxiety, and stress.

2. Sleep improves. Sex relates to a more and better quality of sleep. It is a bonus for the older generation when many individuals are fighting insomnia and awakening during the night.

3. Physical appearance improves. Couples who have sex three times a week look ten years younger, according to research performed by neuropsychologist David Weeks of Scotland's Royal Edinburgh Hospital.[232] This result is possible because of the hormones released during sex, or people who have sex more often, pay more attention to their appearance, diet, and exercise.

4. Vaginal dryness (VD) decreases. Sex can be painful for menopausal women with VD, but it is treatable. Once the dryness has improved, having sex two to three times a week can keep VD away by increasing the blood flow to the vagina, which helps improve lubrication and elasticity of the tissues. The moisture moves through the vagina, keeping it clean and

removing dead cells. The vaginal moisture is slightly acidic, and this condition helps to keep the area healthy, preventing infections such as thrush. Vaginal dryness also occurs due to a drop in the level of estrogen following the removal of ovaries during a hysterectomy or following chemotherapy. Decreased amounts of estrogen also lead to a thinner, less elastic, and more fragile vaginal lining. Doctors can prescribe estrogen vaginal cream that can be used as little as once a week to help with problems of vaginal dryness.

5. Sex improves a woman's bladder control. Sex is like a workout and strengthens the pelvic floor muscles.

6. Men can lower the odds of prostate cancer. Men ages 46 to 81, who frequently ejaculate, twenty-one times a month compared to seven times or fewer, developed much less prostate cancer, found in a study of 29,000 men.[233] Scientists theorize that it is because infrequent ejaculation allows carcinogenic secretions to remain in the prostate. In other words, "cleaning out the pipes" helps to prevent disease.

7. Relationships can be strengthened. Even after forty years of marriage, sexually active pairs consistently report higher levels of marital satisfaction, according to a 2014 study of 500 couples ages 58–85.[234] Sex in this study did not necessarily mean intercourse. Cuddling, hugging, and kissing all help to maintain intimacy, according to University of Chicago sociologist Linda Waite.

8. Pain relief can be a benefit of sexual activity. The activity eases those aches and pains, even if it is only temporary relief. During sex, the hormone oxytocin is produced, leading to an increase in endorphins. The flow of endorphins through the body makes us feel better, emotionally, and physically. Sexual activity and regular exercise encourage the body to produce extra synovial fluid, which can help lubricate joints and make movement less painful. Cardiovascular fitness, strength, and flexibility improve though the act of lovemaking. As with any exercise, getting the blood flowing and the heart pumping is good for circulation.

9. Individuals experience less severe headaches. Sex may help relieve migraine pain, a 2013 study found.[235] A headache specialist at the University of Munster, Germany, surveyed migraine sufferers who had sex during their headaches. 60% said it reduced or halted the pain.

10. Intimacy for seniors improves happiness. Seniors live longer indulging in food, drink, increased socialization, and by remaining sexually active. Intimacy is linked to life satisfaction and longer life in some cases.

11. Sexual activity may trigger immune and inflammatory changes in the body. It helps fight off infections due to improved immune response.

Professor Liu, an Associate Professor of Sociology at Michigan State University, presented the following findings after analyzing national survey data from 2,204 people aged 47 to 85. "Frequent, satisfying, sexual activity poses cardiovascular risks for older men, but regular orgasmic sex could protect aging women from certain problems like hypertension. The stress of exerting the activity to reach an orgasm in males caused an increase in blood pressure and cardiovascular problems."[236] However, at the age of 60, 70, and even 85 years of age, seniors can enjoy active sex lives. The benefits far outweigh any possible negative effects. If you are using protection, you can safely engage in sexual activity. Unfortunately, sexually transmitted diseases have increased among the elderly population due to unprotected sex. The availability of drugs like Viagra, Cialis, Levitra, Staxyn, and Stendra has helped many men from erectile dysfunction. With a partner or self-pleasuring, having sex can improve the quality of your life.

Human beings were not genetically engineered to be monogamous. The concept of the killer sperm ensured that if a woman was having sex with more than one male, the healthiest, most potent sperm would merge with the egg to ensure the birth of the strongest offspring. Maybe that is the reason why DNA testing of humans has become so popular in recent years. The children's parents may not be their biological parents. They are testing their children to ensure that they are indeed their biological offspring, especially in very wealthy families with sizable estates.

Open relationships are just as satisfying as monogamous ones, a University of Guelph study revealed in June 2018. The story made headlines appearing in CTV News, the New York Post, and the Daily Mail. Jessica Wood, a Ph.D. student in applied social psychology and lead author of the study, said: "We found people in consensual, non-monogamous relationships experience the same levels of relationship satisfaction, psychological well-being, and sexual satisfaction as those in monogamous relationships. This theory debunks the societal views of monogamy as being the ideal relationship structure."[237] In consensual, non-monogamous relationships, all partners agree to engage in multiple sexual or romantic relationships. Between three and seven percent of people in North America are currently in a consensually non-monogamous relationship. Wood said: "It is more common than most people think. We are at a point in social history where we are expecting a lot from our partners. We want to have sexual fulfillment and excitement but also emotional and financial support. Trying to fulfill all these needs can put pressure on relationships. To deal with this pressure, we are seeing some people look to consensually non-monogamous relationships.

However, these types of relationships still attract stigma. They are perceived as immoral and less satisfying. It is assumed that individuals in these types of relationships are having sex with everyone all the time. They are villainized and viewed as bad people in bad relationships, but that is not the case."[238] Among the questions, the researchers asked how often the respondents considered separating, whether they confided in their partner, and what was their general level of happiness. "In both monogamous and non-monogamous relationships, people engage in sex to be close to their partner and fulfill their sexual needs. They have a more satisfying relationship than those who have sex for less fundamental reasons, such as to avoid conflict. Ultimately, if you are fulfilling your psychological needs and are satisfied sexually, you are more likely to be happy in your partnership, no matter the relationship structure."[239]

A word of caution here is that both partners must agree with the arrangements. Feelings of being left out and jealousy can cause major heartache and unwanted consequences. Couples who have been together for a long time can stop making the other partner feel special, take the partner for granted, or do not infuse romance in their activities, which leads to complacency. Couples care about each other and have no plans to separate, but just do not get sexually excited by their partners. A consensual non-monogamous relationship is a viable alternative to keep relationships going and maintain happiness.

> *"Life's tragedy is we get old too soon and wise too late."*[240]
>
> *Benjamin Franklin*

For a Better Marriage, Act Like a Single Person

"Don't depend too much on anyone in this world because even your own shadow leaves you when you are in darkness."[241]

Ibn Taymiyyah

Stephanie Coontz is the Director of Research and Public Education for the Council on Contemporary Families and Emeritus Faculty of History and Family Studies at The Evergreen State College in Olympia, Washington, in addition to an author of five books on gender, family and marriage. She was quoted in a New York Times article that your soulmate is no substitute for a social life. In a marital or couple relationship, it is vital for both spouses or partners also to have their own social life.[242] "Maintaining social networks and self-reliance after marriage does far more than protect you against depression and ensures against the worst outcomes of divorce or widowhood. It can also enhance and even revitalize your marriage."[243]

In this era, when both partners in a relationship are working outside the home, they are spending more time apart. It is essential to acquire skills as individuals to be successful. Whether you are single, with a partner, or married, there are significant personal rewards to be gained by fostering independence. "The reality is, 110.6 million Americans ages 18 or older (or 45.2 percent) are single, according to data from the U.S. Census Bureau—a number that's been rising since 2015. People are staying single longer than ever before. In 2018, the highest median ages ever for a first marriage were reported: 30 years for men and 28 years for women."[244] This statistic lowers the risk of getting a divorce. Most divorces occur in individuals between the ages of 20 and 24 years old. 24.6 percent get divorced between the age of 25 and 39. Couples are getting married later in life. Individuals have reached their educational goals, achieved career and financial stability, have developed life skills such as managing a budget, learning to cook, and acquiring some skills at completing household repairs.

Single people have more extensive social networks than married couples, who tend to rely on each other for companionship. They interact more with friends, neighbors, co-workers, and extended family. As individuals, they participate more in clubs, political organizations, teams, unions, churches, and cultural events. This aspect of participation protects them against early mortality. It has been proven that your risk factor for dying young increases with fewer social networks, as compared to the risks of obesity, and leading a sedentary life.[245]

Having a vast network of friends is most beneficial, in addition to family socialization. Today, many families live far apart. It is not always possible or affordable to travel and be together for all the holidays and family celebrations. Unresolved disagreements with family members may be the reason to disassociate from destructive family relationships. Close friends are your extended family; life events can be just as joyful with this network of individuals around you. Harper Lee in *"To Kill a Mockingbird"* wrote: "You can choose your friends, but not your family."[246] She expounded on the value of "your kin," but close friendships are invaluable when family relationships are not positive or available.

> *"Family is not about blood. It is about who is willing to hold your hand when you need it most or who can you depend on to stand by you in the middle of the night when called upon to do so."*[247]
>
> *Author Unknown*

A long-term study in the United Kingdom of more than six thousand five hundred people found that people having ten or more friendships at age forty-five years old, had significantly higher levels of psychological well-being at age fifty, regardless of their partnership status, as compared to people with fewer friends.[248]

William Chopik from Michigan State University completed two other recent studies of nearly two hundred and eighty thousand people in almost one hundred countries. He found that friendships become increasingly vital to well-being at older ages.[249] Relationships with friends are a better predictor of good health and happiness among older adults than relationships with family.

The institution of marriage can provide emotional, financial, and practical support. Having a perfect mate should not be a substitute for pursuing relationships with friends and enjoying interests separate from one another. Partners in marriage can be encouraging and helpful with careers, childrearing, and household chores. They can also be uncooperative in sharing family responsibilities, depending on their different personalities and assumed roles. Some marriages break up; one partner changes and becomes more self-sufficient and fulfilled. The other partner feels he or she has been left behind. Divorces often occur with older couples after the children have left home to pursue their own lives. The wife may attend college to pursue a profession for a new career. The husband feels that his wife is no longer the woman he married. This could cause stress in the relationship. The couple is no longer compatible. Divorces also occur when complacency, routine and boredom set in. Neither one in the relationship feels any excitement or looks forward to sharing events together.

Successful singles make excellent marriage partners and usually end up in happy marriages. On average, studies show that married people are more satisfied with life and live longer than single people. The most distressed single people are the ones who are newly divorced or widowed. This anxiety and pain may stem from an over reliance on one's spouse before the divorce or death of the spouse. The surviving partner appears unable to cope and seems lost without a partner. Only time and maybe therapy will heal the pain. Single individuals with a low income report the most psychological problems. Low income married couples have more resources to draw from their partners. Single people, who become more affluent, foster more relationships and interests compared to married individuals. Those individuals who have remained single with the highest incomes tend to be happier than married couples.

Most marriage counselors tend to focus on improving marital relationships, when in fact, the focus should be on fostering individuality and responsibility for one's happiness.

Partners are happier when their spouses are content and have strong social networks. When problems in the relationship arise, talking with a close friend outside of the marriage can be greatly beneficial. "You are my everything" is not the best recipe for a happy marriage. However, there are a few exceptions. Some couples prefer to do all their socialization with each other. They enjoy the company of their partner to the extent that they may not need other people. This relationship must be acceptable to both partners. However, this arrangement limits the opportunities to meet different people. Socialization with others enhances our daily life experiences.

> *"One smile can start a friendship, one word can end a fight, one look can save a relationship, and one person can change your life."*[250]
>
> *Author Unknown*

Friends with Benefits

Casual sexual encounters require specific rules for it to work. Otherwise, emotions get tangled, and problems arise. Here are some recommendations if you are interested in this type of relationship.

1. Do not be possessive. Do not bombard the individual with texts and snapchats. Do not linger after the encounter.
2. Do not get personal. This relationship is supposed to be a "source of physical fun," not an emotional one.
3. Select someone whom you are attracted to physically. Mental compatibility leads to bonds and the possibility of developing an emotional connection. Spend less time talking and more time "messing around."
4. Time in the bedroom should outweigh all else.
5. Use protection. Be aware of the chances of STDs or AIDs.
6. Set boundaries for your health. Do not agree to perform actions that make you feel uncomfortable.
7. Keep it fun and enjoyable. If you find the sexual encounter to be work and stressful, back off.
8. Keep in mind; you are not dating.
9. Remain cautious. Keep your feelings in check. Most people believe that females have a more difficult time with break-ups, but research shows that men feel more strongly. This may be the case as men tend to keep feelings bottled up, and they do not talk to friends as much as females do. Emoting helps to get rid of negative emotions.

Features that Attract People the Most

1. A study at Manchester University in England found that lips are a woman's most attractive physical attribute. Men with full lips are also admired.
2. Strong eye contact for both sexes. "Eyes are the window to the soul;" however, they are the door to keeping a lover's attention.
3. Men wearing glasses adds charm and is associated with intellect.
4. Thick eyebrows on men creates a rough male look.
5. Bristle or a facial stubble is seen as fashionable on a man.
6. Straight white teeth are more attractive to both sexes.
7. Facial symmetry: most models and celebrities have strong facial and physical attractiveness.
8. Show a happy face. People are more attracted to someone with a sincere smile and laughing eyes.
9. High cheek bones on men makes them look confident and strong.
10. Researchers found that men preferred larger hip to waist ratios in women than smaller body type ratios. However, all body types are beautiful and attractive. Women like a flat, toned stomach on a man. It shows that he pays attention to his body and does not have unhealthy habits.
11. Streaks of grey hair at the temples or grey hair overall for men, gives the impression of being of reasonable age with experience and wisdom.
12. A hair line going up to the belly button is seen as seductive on men.

13. Veins on a man's arms are associated with strength and stamina.

14. Men's natural scent can either be inviting or not. The smell intoxicates some women.

15. Wearing red is more attractive and sexually desirable. Men want to spend more money on females who wear red clothes.

16. Body language, especially turning towards the partner, leaning in, tilting head, and pointing towards the feet, communicate subconsciously interest and engagement. Blushing also signals attraction for both individuals.

17. Confidence is the key! Confident people are more apt to send off signals of interest. If you send out more signs, you get more in return. Having the mindset that you are happy with who you are, helps to make a better impression than someone with low self-esteem.

18. Self-awareness, "know yourself." Understanding your internal state, preferences, resources, and intuitions help. Also, be aware of your needs, desires, failings, habits, likes, dislikes, and non-negotiables. What are you willing to do? What makes you angry, defensive, or happy?

19. Being more self-aware can significantly improve self-confidence. It enables us to see our strengths and weaknesses.

20. Authenticity is essential to have realistic perceptions of ourselves and our partner. The following traits are essential for this type of relationship: accepting of oneself and others, behaving thoughtfully, possessing a non-hostile sense of humor, expressing emotions freely, being open to learning from mistakes, and understanding. All these behaviors allow

people to be honest about who they are and comfortable about who they are not.

21. People are genuine without pretenses. Demonstrating an honest self-perception of yourself will build a deeper, more meaningful connection with others. Quirks are endearing to those who know you and love you. Authenticity will be most attractive to those who do not know you!

Samantha Joel, professor at Western University in London Ontario, and her colleagues analyzed information from more than 11,000 couples for a study that explored what makes relationships successful.[251] The study revealed that the quality of the relationship rather than individual personalities of the couple dictated how satisfied they were in the relationship. The characteristics that best predicted a person's satisfaction were perceived partner satisfaction and commitment, appreciation for each other, sexual satisfaction, and conflict resolution. On the other hand: life satisfaction, attachment avoidance or anxiety, negative affect and depression were the best individual predictors for relationship dissatisfaction. Another conclusion drawn from the study was "how you feel now can be somewhat diagnostic of how you'll feel later on" as the same pattern was found at follow-up.

Why Men Stay Single?

The University of Nicosia in Cyprus published a research article in August 2018, analyzing why men choose to remain single.[252] In Western societies, a substantial portion of the adult population does not have an intimate partner. In the United States, a Gallup survey found that 64% of adults in the age group 18–29 were identified as single and had never married. In 2015, in the United Kingdom, 34.5% of the adult population was identified as single. These individuals had never cohabited or married, as reported by the Office of National Statistics in 2016. Eurostat, a statistical office of the European Union situated in Luxembourg, provides high- quality statistics for Europe. It is estimated that single-person households accounted for 31.7% of the private households within the 28 countries of the European Union in 2015. In Canada, a 2016 census indicated that one-person domiciles accounted for 28.2% of all family units. Another American study determined that 32.7% of the adult population was not in a committed relationship. The prevalence of these single household rates leads to the question to understand why so many people are single. Two main factors contribute to this phenomenon: it is by choice, and individuals face difficulties in attracting a partner.

Studies point to poor flirting skills while trying to attract someone as the main reason preventing people from finding a partner. To reproduce, individuals must get together with the opposite sex. Sexual desire and romantic love may help to motivate, attract, and retain mates. The primary evolutionary purpose of mating is to have children. Children require considerable parental investment before they can reach maturity and survive on their own. It would be most beneficial for people not to mate randomly. They need to be selective and search for mates who will be helpful to them and avoid those individuals who do not possess the necessary qualities for a mutual and positive relationship. In Western societies, individuals want partners who are reliable with employment. They prefer someone who is educated and can provide for a family. After acquiring these skills and qualities, it is an excellent time to search out a person with qualifications that are attractive and beneficial to you. Good looks constitute a quality that is highly valued. Good-looking men may choose not to commit to long-term relationships, and instead, choose to have many different casual relationships.

Overall, there are three main reasons why individuals remain single. They are focused on obtaining a good education or a good job to become financially independent. Men want to enjoy more freedom, have casual partners, and advance their careers. There are restrictions to one's lifestyle once married and benefits to being healthy and single. There may be sexual issues, homosexuality, poor health, mental health, disability, or addiction problems, which give men reasons to remain single. Other issues include poor looks, especially baldness and short stature but personality traits and good mannerisms can boost confidence. Previous relationships were bad experiences, or they were unable to get over the last break-up, which creates fear of rejection. Children from a previous marriage may give pause to starting a new relationship. Others may be shy, introverted, have low self-esteem or are socially awkward, so are unable to initiate contact with women. Other men have different priorities and are just not interested or do not have enough time to pursue relationships.

Men reported they had trouble approaching women and picking up on cues from women who are interested in them. They feel uncomfortable initiating a conversation. Regrettably, even if some men want a relationship with a woman, they do not make the efforts to find a partner. Formerly in many societies, fathers controlled their sons and daughters, and selected spouses for their children. Since parents no longer find partners for their children, they remain single. In the past, when parents did choose partners for their children, looks were not of paramount importance. Many men are single due to their obesity, poor looks, and grooming. Some men are unreasonably particular. They go after women whom they will never be able to get. They simply do not know how to select an appropriate long-term partner.

Social factors may also play a part in this selection process. Exposure to movies, television series, and commercials depicts unrealistically good-looking individuals. This media exposure may result in men having a skewed view of what constitutes the characteristics of being handsome. These same viewpoints can affect how men feel about the size of their penises, especially if there is overexposure to pornographic material. The men starring in these venues have above average size penises. Men may form unrealistic points of reference as to what is normal.

With the anger generated by the #MeToo Movement, men are going to struggle, even more, especially those already having trouble saying the right things or behaving in a manner that can attract women of their choice. Men are experiencing many personal issues of their own, which they are trying to overcome. Women's display of anger in the workplace simply adds fuel to the fire, where men may feel overwhelmed and anxious. Many men have reported that they viewed singlehood as a negative state which they wanted to escape but have trouble finding a partner. When they were receiving an education or getting established in their careers, it was a favorable state. Once they secured a good job, they felt stressed being single. The pressures include social and financial commitments, and most of all, loneliness. Being single is not a permanent state. Eventually, most people do meet someone with whom they can settle down. Many men do experience prolonged periods of being alone, and if they face extended difficulties in meeting a partner, remaining single may become a permanent state.

In a recent article in The Economic Times, "Five Benefits of Dating Smart Women," the latest research claimed that while men say they would rather date brains over beauty, they choose the opposite characteristic in a woman.[253] Why? A man's ego cannot handle a woman who is more intelligent than himself. However, he is not making the right decision. Unless the man himself is highly intelligent, he is automatically discounting millions of women available for long-term relationships. He should not be intimidated by intelligent women, as there are benefits to dating smart and strong women.

The man will not get bored. There is always something to talk about with a smart woman. She understands a lot about the world and how it works. A couple usually spends a great deal of time in their relationship discussing things, not just having sex. Having an intelligent partner makes life interesting.

The woman may earn a higher salary. This conclusion is not always the case, but women can be more ambitious and highly educated. The man may not be able to give up his job and stay home, but an increase in household income is a positive attribute.

Women may be more adventurous. An intelligent mind does not want to sit in front of the television every evening. She will be more open to going out and experiencing new things. She will be more independent and self-reliant.

The woman may challenge the man to improve himself through education and life choices. If she is intelligent and ambitious, she will not put up with any excuses from a man. He will be forced to accept responsibilities and increase the well-being of the relationship, a partnership.

The woman will probably take better care of herself. She may be less likely to smoke, take drugs, drink, or overeat. She may be more likely to exercise. The man will hopefully want to keep up physical fitness with his partner. A couple who values a healthy lifestyle together forms a strong relationship.

Robinson Meyer from *The Atlantic* reported a new online dating study whose results showed that everyone aspires to date other people out of their league.[254] When a person meets someone they might be attracted to, their initial reaction may be to forget it since that person may be smarter, wealthier, younger, or of a higher social class than themselves. Even Prince Harry from the UK had said he needed "to up his game" when he first met Meghan Markle! Elizabeth Bruch, a sociology professor at the University of Michigan, reports that three-quarters or more people are dating aspirationally.[255] Users of online dating sites spend most of their time trying to contact people "out of their league." They found that in most contacts, more than 80% are the men who establish the first contact. Bruch emphasized that the hierarchy did not depend on race, age, or educational level, but it is derived from user behavior. The response "captures whatever traits people are replying to when they pursue partners. These traits include wittiness, genetic factors, or whatever interest people to send out messages."[256] She concluded that people should realize that the reply rate is low, between zero and ten%, but they should keep sending out messages. The key was to be persistent.

The main conclusion from the study is not very encouraging. Men's desirability peaks at ages 40 to 50 and stays flat over the age distribution. Women's desirability starts high at age 18 and falls throughout their lifespan. Hence, older women have a harder time in the dating market. Women's prospects dim not only as they age, but also as they achieve the highest level of education. A more educated man is almost always more desirable. However, for women, an undergraduate degree is most beneficial. Postgraduate education is associated with decreased desirability among women.

When men lose their wives through divorce or death, they seem to have an easier time dating and getting married again, in comparison to when women lose their spouses.[257] After losing a spouse in middle age, 54% of men, compared to only 7% of women were in a romantic relationship a year later. Among older adults, who lost a spouse, 15% of men were dating after six months, compared with less than 1% of women. After two years, 25% of men had remarried, compared with 5% of women. Society has placed different expectations of men and women's dating habits after the loss of their spouses. It is more acceptable for men to start new relationships, but women are expected to grieve for a more extended period. On a more practical level, the responsibility falls more heavily on women to care for children and aging parents. Women are also handicapped due to financial reasons, as well as time constraints.

Discrimination against widows occurs worldwide, especially in countries like India, China, Turkey, South Korea, and Nigeria. As mentioned earlier, widows in India had to commit "sati" before this practice was banned. However, in some parts of India, widows are cast out by their own families, left to beg to survive even today. There is an excellent movie entitled "Water" produced by an Indian female film director, Deepa Mehta, who examines the plight of a group of widows who are forced into poverty following the deaths of their husbands. As an aside, she made two other movies, an "elemental" trilogy of *Water, Fire and Earth*, addressing Indian women's issues.

Dating and meeting potential partners have become more complicated over time since arranged marriages are becoming less popular. It is no surprise that most people find their partners in their workplace. #MeToo Movement is going to decrease chances of this happening as well. Most people will be afraid to flirt or make any moves. Most companies are effectively banning what used to be normal social behaviors. People who lack confidence within themselves will continue to struggle with loneliness unless they reach out to people who are being seen as less desirable. Until you get to know someone well, it is difficult to judge their actual assets or faults. Psychologists have found that over time, people usually regret their missed chances, not the opportunities they took. You regret the things you do not do, not the challenges you did take.

Maybe this is why people fall in and out of love so often, given the high divorce rate. Some say people do not fall in love anymore. They just find a temporary attachment with an individual who entertains them. Some people may not recognize love; they think that they are having a brief fling. And then, they fall in love. The world does not go around on entertainment. People need love to fuel their passion.

> *"Some people may be brokenhearted not because they have been hurt but because they have never found someone who mattered enough to hurt them."*[258]
>
> *André Aciman*

Hope for Women and Society

How can there not be hope?

A man is born through a woman.

A woman raises him.

He falls in love with a woman. (There are exceptions with the gay community.)

He marries a woman.

It is surprising to find a man who does not respect a woman.

Women may not be physically as strong as men. However, women at times have no choice but to keep going, especially in the caretaking role. For example, when the whole family is infected with the flu virus, the mother is the one who takes care of all her sick children, her husband and herself. After putting up with oppression from men in most societies, women still have the tenacity to want to overcome these problems and improve the human race. After all, only women can continue to produce offspring (until the time of test-tube babies). Since the beginning of time, women have been considered to be a stronger race. Most men would not be able to tolerate the pain of childbirth! Women have taken on the brunt of raising children, doing all the mundane things like cooking, cleaning, laundry, driving children back and forth to school, and extra-curricular activities. They are the ones who take care of the children, the sick, and the elderly in the home for the most part. It has been this way for generations, but the millennials may be putting a dent in this way of life. The men may be stepping up to the plate to help more and not feel like they are being de-masculinized by taking on the role that was traditionally filled by women. In my own family, it has been interesting to see my nephew, (who grew up in an Indian culture where males are treated special, and women take care of them,) take on many responsibilities of childcare, babysitting, cooking, cleaning, and work at his successful business. In contrast, his wife, a successful career woman, can focus on her job and share in the household and childcare chores when she can.

Once limited to poor women and minorities, single motherhood is becoming the new "norm." This prevalence of single parenthood is due in part to the growing trend of children being born outside of marriage, a social pattern that was virtually unheard-of decades ago. About four out of ten children are born to unwed mothers. Nearly two-thirds of children were born to single mothers under the age of 30, according to the Centers for Disease Control (CDC) in 2015.[259] Today, 1 in 4 children under the age of 18, a total of about 17.2 million children, are being raised without a father.[260] According to the U.S. Census Bureau, out of 12 million single-parent families with children under the age of 18, more than 80% were headed by single mothers.[261] Around half of the single mothers have never married. About 42% are White, 33% Black, and 25% Hispanic. At any time, 77.6% of single women are working outside the home. According to the U.S. Bureau of Labor Statistics, this is a slightly higher rate than 69.9% married mothers working outside of the home.[262]

Women have been able to multitask much better than men due to the requirement of getting things done both at home and work. For the most part, males focus on work and their careers, inventions, etc. Women are fortunate; they are given the choice of being a homemaker, a career person, or both livelihoods. Some men have the same choice as well. Some workplaces can accommodate women or men working from home. Their work can be performed remotely, completing work assignments despite having home responsibilities. Partners have learned how to cooperate to increase their family's income. Some families can even afford hired help to assist with family responsibilities such as childcare and housework.

We are at a point in our culture where women must be allowed to make a choice, without apologies, if they choose not to marry or have children. Women need to permit themselves to feel free, unencumbered with their lifestyle choices. *NOT ALL WOMEN WANT TO GET MARRIED OR NEED TO HAVE CHILDREN.* Society thinks that there is something wrong if a woman chooses not to marry, is unable to or is unwilling to have or raise children. Women especially need to stop shaming other women for the choices they make.

My father believed strongly in education and insisted that all his three daughters must obtain higher education and have a career. At the time, this belief in educating young women was radical thinking within Indian families. Daughters were raised to be married off through arranged marriages by their early 20s at the very latest. My mother always regretted that she only had a high school education. My mother did not learn to drive and was dependent on my father for her welfare. My mother's mantra to us was to study hard, have a career, and never choose to be dependent on your husband, especially if you are unhappy in your marriage.

Well, guess what! I took my parent's advice to heart. I studied hard, became a physician, and married my boyfriend after completing medical school. My marriage was ideal; we were in love. We were both physicians, compatible friends, and our families got along very well. At times life throws you a curveball to see how you will survive. The stress of hectic private practices took its toll on our married life. We separated for two years before getting a divorce. Culturally at this time, it was not considered appropriate for Indian couples to divorce. Indian women were raised to bear all injustices, and you simply did not leave your husband, especially if he was not abusing you, was not an alcoholic, a gambler or drug addict. And if he made a very decent living and was conservative with his spending, even the more reasons to remain married to him.

During that time, all my feel-good neurotransmitters (dopamine and serotonin) were depleted. I broke all the Indian societal, cultural traditions with which I had been raised. It was a challenging time for me. Despite being in a successful career as a physician, I felt like a failure. I was not happy in my marriage; I could not have children. The woman in an Indian marriage is expected to give birth and have offspring to continue her husband's family name. I recall thinking: the phoenix must rise from its ashes. I became emotionally stronger after ending my marriage. I continued to have a highly successful career. People in my community did not shun me because I was a divorced, professional woman. My parents were only concerned about my happiness. I dated and decided to cohabitate with a

Caucasian man, the first White male in our family. We have been together 30 plus years.

I have shared some of my personal life to show you how many cultural norms I have broken. There is plenty of hope for women to break out of the expectations imposed by society and achieve whatever you choose to accomplish. Marry someone only if it makes sense to do so, and you are happy and satisfied. Never marry because you think that it is what society expects of you. You can always form a bond and commit to your friend, boyfriend, lover, soulmate, or partner without marrying. Find a partner with whom you are compatible and have a deep friendship. This partner in life should also be willing to help in the home with all chores and responsibilities, especially if you choose to have a career outside the home. Be highly respectful of one another. Learn how to fully trust one another, so you can tell each other anything without fear of repercussions or reprisals. These lessons are easier said than done but learn how to be honest with one another. In your relationship, be true to yourself.

Couples always have expectations of each other, and it is difficult to just "live and let live." There will be conflicts if both partners are not responsible or if one takes advantage of the other. Sheryl Sandberg stated in her book *Lean In*, "culture teaches all of us that men should achieve, and women should support others. The truth is that everyone should achieve, and everyone should support others." [263]

"Relations are like electric currents. Wrong connection will give you shocks throughout your life, but the right ones will light up your life".[264]

Ravi Soni

By all means, have children if you want a family. Do not have children because you want to leave a part of yourself on this earth when you turn to dust. That is just being egocentric. Do not be fooled into thinking that these adorable children will grow up to be responsible adults and will take care of you when you are old. There will be a lot of joys and tears on that journey, and at the end of the day, make sure you have enough financial resources to take care of yourself in your old age. The world's wealthiest individuals, those with a net worth of at least $5 Million, will be passing down $15.4 Trillion of wealth to the next generation by 2030, with more than half of those assets transferred within North America.[265] People need to take care of themselves because children often have other ideas about what to do with their inheritance.

Men and women can be equal on many different levels, but we cannot be the same. Men have to be allowed to be men. They should not impose the old cultural expectations on women whose role in society is changing drastically. Women themselves need to take responsibility for not being overly dependent on men. They must work with men to help them learn how to be more active with household chores and childcare. The Millennials are already making the transition of sharing these tasks. Women who choose to be homemakers and not pursue a career, take those responsibilities very seriously. They need to take care of the home, their husband or partner and the children.

Relating to divorce, you hear so often about women who did not contribute economically to the marriage, or in maintaining the household, yet they walk away with almost everything. They had been dependent on their husband during the years of their marriage. As women, let us learn to be fair and not let emotions make us greedy and unreasonable, thinking that we must teach men a lesson. It is true; men often leave their wives and children for younger women. Just look at the statistics on single-parent households in the United States. Courts tend to be generous to women in these divorce settlements. However, women receive a terrible reputation for wanting to take men to the cleaners for being scorned and replaced.

Women need to be honest, take pride in themselves, believe in their abilities to function on their own if divorce is inevitable. They need to be strong enough to let things go that make them unhappy. It is so vital for them to obtain higher education or vocational training after high school, so if a divorce is evident, women can take care of themselves. Women want equality. They need to accept responsibility for themselves, instead of playing the role of being the weak individual in the relationship. There are always consequences when one's life is turned upside down.

> *"All changes, even the most longed for, have their melancholy, for what we leave behind us is a part of ourselves. We must die to one life before we can enter another."*[266]
>
> Anatole France (1844-1924)

Women sometimes claim to be abused by men without any proof. Men have truly little recourse to address these accusations as women tend to be believed, leaving men in a very precarious situation. There are many incidents where men are mentally or physically abused by women. It is not "manly" to report such incidents. If they try to stop the women from attacking them, the women, in turn, shout even louder that they are being abused, although they may have started the confrontation. In such cases, my advice is for men to walk away, file charges, do whatever they need to do to clear their name. Otherwise, events may escalate against them, primarily if women are determined to ruin their reputation or blackmail them into giving them whatever they want. Just as women need to stand up to being abused and not tolerate it, the same recommendation goes for men.

It is incredible how often people think they are in love and cannot live without their partner. They get married without thinking through all that is involved in establishing and maintaining a healthy relationship. No one wants to be treated cruelly when the bond is broken, and it ends in divorce. Do people fall out of love the instant they find out their partner has cheated on them since affairs are the main reason for so many divorces? The word "love" seems to be used very loosely without really understanding its meaning. Couples need to try to understand why this situation happened and remember why they got married in the first place. Affairs usually arise out of unmet needs. If both people do not work together to keep each other happy, end up taking their partner for granted, become self-absorbed, or spend more time with other people and activities, the relationship will suffer. If one individual stays healthy, exercises regularly, and wants to look and feel their best, while the other partner becomes old, complaining about their health issues without investing time for self-improvement, the couple will be headed for trouble. If conflicts over children or elderly parents are not resolved together, this situation can also lead to an incredibly stressful relationship. If the couple does not address these difficulties together, one or both partners will start looking for someone else outside this primary relationship for comfort and understanding.

> *"Relationships are not exams to pass or fail and not a competition to win or lose. It is a feeling in which you care for someone more than yourself."*[267]
>
> *Buddha's Teaching & Science*

Women should not feel guilty if they break tradition and pursue a career, instead of getting married, having children, and a job. Women believe that men plan their careers for decades with few responsibilities related to family household management. Women have to factor in family, children, household chores, in addition to managing their careers. Career women should expect and demand equality in the workplace. They should not play the race or sex card when things do not go well at work. Their energy is better expended in finding solutions. Sometimes, women must work harder to prove themselves in a male-dominated field. It is not fair, but that is the reality at work today. This work climate needs to be overcome, but the rewards will be well worth their efforts.

The medical field was male-dominated career path at one time. Now more women are applying to medical schools and gaining admission. The women have proven that they can put in the required hours to become successful physicians. Female doctors have earned the trust of their patients. They are better listeners, more compassionate, and demonstrate the ability to meet their patients' emotional needs. In an overall satisfaction survey, more patients express satisfaction and choose female physicians over their male counterparts.[268]

On August 26, 1920, the US Secretary of State certified that the 19th Amendment to the Constitution had been ratified by the required 36 states. It became the law of the land. "The right of citizens of the United States to vote shall not be denied or abridged by the United States or by any State on account of sex." It was a hundred years ago this year, in 2020, that women finally got the right to vote. However, the women who showed up to register to vote in the fall of 1920 confronted many hurdles. Racism was the most significant one. Despite many setbacks, women are on equal footing now in their ability to make their voices heard with no barriers regarding casting their votes.

I want to believe that there is hope for women, especially considering all the changes that may come about with the #MeToo Movement. Hopefully, men will be more sensitive in understanding the needs of women. In turn, women will remain truthful and understand how men think and function.

In 2018, the Indian film "Pad Man," a biographical drama debuted on Netflix. The story is about a South Indian man named Laxmi, who gets married and loves his wife dearly. As was customary in the village, his wife was temporarily banished from the household during her menstrual periods. Laxmi had truly little knowledge about this subject but was worried when he saw his wife hanging up the soiled rags on the washing line, which she used during her periods. When he asked his wife about it, she responded that it was not his concern. Undeterred, Laxmi went to the store and bought her sanitary pads, which cost 55 Rupees. When he returned home and handed the package to his wife, she reprimanded him and told him to return the costly napkins. The price was equivalent to their milk expenses for the month. He was unable to return the package, and his wife was unwilling to use the pads.

He did find a use for them when a co-worker was injured and able to stop the bleeding. The doctor at the hospital told Laxmi that this was the cleanest way to tend to the wound. The doctor had also informed him that women were getting infections, some leading to infertility, and even death from using the "dirty cloth rags" during their menstrual cycles. Excited, Laxmi bought cotton, cloth, and glue. He made a temporary pad, which he thought would work as well as the expensive pad for his wife. The pad he made did not work. Laxmi persisted in trying to improve the product. His wife still refused to try any of his pads. He asked a young neighbor girl and some female medical students to try them. This action further alienated his wife. The neighbors accused him of chasing women and having an affair. He even obtained some goat blood and tried the pad himself with a disastrous outcome of blood-stained pants in public. Laxmi was labeled a "pervert" by the whole village. His wife returned to her pre-marital home. He was forced to leave the town and move away.

He ended up working at a professor's house since he needed to earn a living and required shelter. The professor's young son introduced Laxmi to the Internet. After learning that the sanitary pads use a more absorbent cellulose fiber than cotton, and after two years of research and findings, Laxmi learned how to procure the exact materials he needed, and the process of manufacturing a viable sanitary pad at home. Laxmi was able to get a sample of the cellulose, and the professor showed him videos of pad-making machines. The machines were costly to buy, so Laxmi built his own pad-making machine. He managed to make a near-perfect pad, but no women would test it.

One day, a group of women was passing by in a car, and one of the women was in desperate need of a sanitary pad, Laxmi gave her one. The next day, he asked the woman for feedback on his invention. She said that it was just as good as the ones sold in the store. After hearing his story, this woman invited him to an innovation fair in Delhi. The winner would be awarded 200,000 Rupees. Laxmi's invention was recognized as the "Life-changing Innovation of the Year." He became famous, but the simple-minded villagers still shamed him for his invention. He refused to sell the patent to big companies because they would increase the cost of the pad and pay huge patent fees. Instead, he chose to make more low-cost pad-making machines. He hired rural women to operate these machines, make the pads, and sell them. In this way, he found a way to keep millions of women safe in India and provide affordable sanitary pads, while empowering many women to have a trade and earn a living.

This movie was based on a true story about Arunachalam Muruganantham, a school drop- out from Tamil Nadu, India. He had made it his life's mission to provide low-cost sanitary napkins to poor women across rural India, where menstruation is still spoken of like a shameful secret. He was invited to New York and gave a speech at UNICEF headquarters. Muruganantham is also known as "India's Menstrual Man." He has lectured at Harvard, at IITs and IIMs in India. He has also spoken with Bill Gates and James Cameron. His low-cost sanitary pad-making machines are now sold across India and are even produced internationally. In 2014, Time magazine featured Muruganantham as one of the "100 Most Influential People in the World." He and his wife are back together.

Why does this story give hope to women? In a conservative country like India, where the needs of poor women are so high, Muruganantham pushed through so much negativity and offered opportunity and empowerment to these women. Can you imagine what could be possible for women in more advanced countries?

"Always try to have eyes that see the best in people, a heart that forgives the worst, a mind that forgets the bad, and a soul that never loses the faith in the goodness of people."[269]

Author Unknown

Last Thoughts to Ponder

Since we are nearing the end of this journey, I feel the need to address some issues that skeptics may raise. They may think that since I have not experienced abuse or discrimination to any extent, I may not know what the #MeToo Movement women are genuinely feeling and experiencing. Suffice to say that I was exposed to inappropriate behavior at a young age leaving me confused. I was also in a short-term, abusive relationship with a "family friend" at the age of 16, followed by other sexually charged issues that plagued my growing-up years. Even though I was a well-established physician, my profession did not shield me from some sexual harassment and comments from my colleagues. I have spoken to other female physicians who have also been in very compromising situations. Their jobs and promotions were jeopardized, if they did not give in to the sexual favors asked of them. All this abusive behavior hits home in a very personal and professional way. I am very aware that sexual harassment transcends all levels of society. Many of my female patients came to me dealing with sexual abuse issues. I had to guide them through the emotional turmoil and hopefully lead them to a place where they were more at peace with themselves and their perpetrators.

"Our personal journeys are an endless well of inspiration and resilience."[270]
Ai-jen Poo, Executive Director for National Domestic Workers Alliance

Since I have shared my sexual harassment history, I would also like to explain the racial discrimination that I have experienced. At the age of 13, my father took our family on a trip through South Africa. At that time, apartheid was the political and social system in South Africa while under white minority rule. The word apartheid means "apartness" in Afrikaans. Racial segregation had been practiced for centuries, but when the new policy started in 1948, it was strict and more systematic.

My father took us to visit a series of caves that were a tourist attraction. We had a separate entrance from the one that the white tourists used. As Indians, we were classified as "colored." While the white tours started often, we had to wait in the heat for a couple of hours before our tour started. Inside the cave system, we had to walk in a line together, away from the other people. A tour guide from one of the "white persons" tour came over to the group and pulled me aside, thinking I was white. I was very fair-skinned and had light-colored hair. "Mzungu toto, come this way." (White child, come this way.) He took me to where the white people were standing. I was able to tell him that I was with the Indians and remained with my parents. During the rest of the tour through South Africa, my family teased me. I would have been able to tour many more parks and areas where only white people were permitted. I could get away for passing as a white person, whereas they would not have been able to enter these places.

There was an active hate group called the "Dotbusters" in the United Kingdom after a number of Indians immigrated to the UK after the decolonization of the African countries. Some of the British young people blamed the Indians for taking away their jobs. This group was most active from 1985–1993. Gang members belonging to this particular hate organization committed hate crimes against Indian people. I had never been exposed to these crimes while living in the UK. However, in 1990, my husband and I went back to visit the University of St. Andrews in Scotland, where we attended medical school. One evening, after watching a movie, we were walking back to the hotel, and a few young men started shouting, "Dotbusters." They began to come towards us in a threatening manner. We were terrified. Fortunately, we were able to get away unharmed.

> *"Anger begins in the minds of human beings,*
> *so it is in the minds of human beings that we*
> *must plant seeds of peace."*[271]
>
> *Dalai Lama*

It is truly disgraceful that people judge others by the color of their skin or gender and intimidate them. Education and tolerance about other cultures must begin at a young age, so children do not grow up with prejudice. Americans are a melting pot of many different cultures from all over the world. Everyone can learn and appreciate the goodness of different people and their ideas.

I want to challenge all females not to think of themselves just as women, but as human beings capable of doing anything once they are determined. This thought process requires dedication and tenacity, and the support from people around you, like your parents, teachers, coaches, friends, lovers, companions, and husbands. Women need to take charge and stop giving into expectations that are outdated by cultural norms.

> *"We all must learn to be open-minded and ready to revise our understanding and belief system. What nurtures me every day on a practical level are my parents, who are my personal heroes and inveterate cheerleaders. They remind me often of my capabilities. They provide me with a broader viewpoint and have always encouraged me to take the high road when I was involved in some petty issue. Their unwavering faith in my capabilities has been my bedrock."*[272]
>
> *Yale University Astrophysicist Priyamvada*
> *Natarajan*

My challenge to men is to respect all females. We may not be able to get to the right place until men stop thinking the crude, insensitive thoughts that give rise to the remarks, even when they are by themselves with other men. This way, there is no reason to hurt women's feelings. Give women their due respect, instead of thinking of them as the weaker race, individuals who cannot accomplish things and are to be exploited. Women were not simply put on this earth to serve and cater to men, run a household, raise children, and take care of the elderly. If partners share the responsibilities, both individuals can be happy, and a lot more can be accomplished. Women bring a whole new set of ideas and perspectives to the table, which can improve performance.

We need to change our culture. The only way that this will happen is with men and women working together. Communication is paramount to solve problems. It has been described that we are still at the "bomb-throwing point" of this revolution. Anger can start a revolution; it cannot negotiate the more delicate steps necessary for real social change. Private conversations, which cannot be legislated or enforced, are essential. This is the kind of challenge predicted by the futurist John Naisbitt, for the human mind.

> *"The most exciting breakthroughs of the 21st century will not occur because of technology, but because of an expanding concept of what it means to be human."*[273]
>
> *John Naisbitt*

I was born in the Rift Valley in Kenya, East Africa. I was brought up in a conservative, male-dominated Indian household, subjected to high cultural expectations, moving through two continents before settling in the "promised land" of America. I was able to rise above all of these obstacles to have a successful life. Women and men can achieve great things in open- minded cultures. They should also have the choice to excel and succeed in a career. I realize that some students cannot secure funds in this country, the United States, to pursue higher education. The government and the higher education establishments need to do a better job providing funds for students, so no young people are left behind who want to study or obtain a skill.

It is imperative to stop focusing on issues from the past. People must be more forgiving and tolerant so that society can move forward. The relationship between men and women needs to be preserved and improved. Most people are tired of hearing about the #MeToo Movement. It has lost its initial empathy and luster. Men and women must be held responsible for their inappropriate behaviors. There is now a higher standard for all of us to observe and respect.

Sexual abuse and harassment issues have been brought to the forefront. It is time to find solutions and move forward. Do not get involved in unnecessary conflicts. Learn to appreciate the contributions that men and women have made to get us to where we are today. Do not sweep everything good under the rug that someone has done because they acted irresponsibly sometime during their life. If people are to be judged only by the negative things that they have done, there will be no positive role models. We all must ask ourselves if we are not guilty of some past transgressions. We are human.

I hope that I have made you aware of specific issues and increased your ability to analyze these subject matters from another viewpoint. Mine is a small voice crying out to the powers that be, whether political, economic, or religious leaders to take immediate steps to find solutions to these catastrophic cultural events and improve the well-being of all citizens. And to young adults, may I recommend that you do everything you can to save our planet from annihilation. Significant changes need to be made soon, or our earth will perish under the perils of climate change. My recommendation to parents is to instill ethical values in your children. Please do not give them everything that they want. Make them into kind, responsible human beings. Teach them how to be productive and appreciate what they have. Be their guiding parents, not just their friends. They will have plenty of friends, but only one set of parents. My advice to the baby boomers is to keep moving, exercising the brain and body. And along the way, try to impart wisdom from the past to whoever will listen. The politicians in the United States need to remember that they work for everybody in the country, not just their party affiliates. They need to stop wasting millions of dollars on elections, and instead, put the money to better causes that are too many to list here.

We all have an expiration date. What will your thoughts be when your end of time arrives? After my father's passing, I went to see his financial manager. We were discussing some of my father's business affairs that he had wrapped up before his passing. I will never forget the words he used when he spoke about my father: "He finished well." These words have stuck in my mind as I too, want "to finish well," when my time comes. I wonder how many of us will be able to say that we did all we could to make the lives of other people we cared about, a little easier after we are gone.

> *"To give of one's self; to leave the world a bit better, whether by a healthy child, a garden patch, or a redeemed social condition; to have played and laughed with enthusiasm and sung with exaltation; to know that even one life has breathed easier because you have lived-this is to have succeeded."*[274]
> *Ralph Waldo Emerson (1803-1882)*

Acknowledgements

First, I need to thank my parents for instilling in me a sense of responsibility and tenacity to undertake the challenge of writing this book. However, it would never have come to fruition if my close friend Robert Koeneman, had not insisted that I write it. The book is mainly his vision to make people think and make the best decisions for humanity to move forward. His concerns about humans destroying themselves gave rise to ideas for this book, and his constant encouragement helped me complete the task. He spent endless hours helping me navigate the computer glitches and educated me in the art of using a computer and not treating it like a typewriter! His belief that I could help people understand different viewpoints, spurred me on to gather ideas and to present them in the book.

Thank you, Hari Zwander, for introducing me to the book, *The Alchemist by Paulo Coelho.* After reading this book, I started thinking that maybe I could put some ideas and concerns down on paper, which might help people struggling with issues that are so troubling in the current era.

Michele Gottlieb, a librarian, and a French professor at the College of Central Florida, threw me a lifeline after reading this book. She understood and was enthusiastic about the American cultural issues and associated problems that I wanted to analyze. Her constant encouragement and vision for this book gave me confidence to continue, and with her help, the manuscript became more fluid and concise. With all her energy and enthusiasm, she inspired me to work harder, persevere, and enhance the book's quality. She became the wind beneath my wings and kept me motivated. I owe her immense gratitude for all her help.

Next, I have a deep appreciation for many friends who read the book and gave their input and editing advice. Dennis Jenkins, who worked as a contractor to NASA for 33 years and was involved in the Air and Space Museums, both in California and Kennedy Space Center in Florida, has authored many books. He took time away from his writing to give me much needed input and direction. He made me understand the need to edit and continue reediting.

Mark George, a former colleague from my time in Valdosta, was very gracious to read the book and spend time giving me feedback on what improvements were needed to engage the reader. Jay Hood, a very successful businessman and an avid reader, immediately understood the significance of the material in the book and was very encouraging in wanting to get the book published. He echoed my sentiments that this book had the potential to make readers think and obtain help for those looking for direction. Donald Pakosh, another businessman, was also very enthusiastic in wanting to help get the book published. Paul Miller, a retired teacher originally from Barbados, immigrated to Manchester, U.K., and now living in California, read the book over a weekend and gave me confidence that I had a good roadmap to help people heal.

Susie Wenstrome, a retired lawyer, spent time pointing out areas that needed improvement and provided redirection in specific chapters. Thank you to Judy Toscano, Jennifer Brand, Gloria Ragonetti, Angela Paporello, Nancy Bray and Kris Kalidindi, who read the book and provided feedback. When I was beginning to write, some other individuals also helped with their suggestions: Lori Rohm, Valerie Robinson, Claire Brew, and her sister Susan Rehwald.

Finally, I want to thank my partner of 30 years, Stephen Ryals, who remains a constant source of support, and I appreciate all he does to help, encourage, and believe in me.

Endnotes

A Personal Journey

[1] "Purna Swaraj: The Demand for Full Independence 26 January 1930," *India of the Past*, accessed September 1, 2019, https://www.indiaofthepast.org/contribute-memories/read-contributions/major-events-pre-1950/283-purna-swaraj-the--the-demand-for-full-independence-26-january-1930.

[2] Sujatha, "Five favorite Speeches by Mahatma Gandhi," *Maps of India*, updated October 1, 2019, published October 2, 2019, accessed October 4, 2019, https://www.mapsofindia.com/my-india/society/5-famous-speeches-of-mahatma-gandhi.

[3] "1942 Quit India Movement," *The Open University*, accessed October 4, 2019, http://www.open.ac.uk/researchprojects/makingbritain/content/1942-quit-india-movement.

[4] "1947 Indian Independence Act," *Parliament United Kingdom*, accessed October 4, 2019, https://www.parliament.uk/about/livingheritage/evolutionofparliament/legislativescrutiny/parliament-and-empire/collections1/collections2/1947-indian-independence-act/.

5 Editors of the Encyclopaedia Britannica, "Mau Mau Kenyan Political Movement," *Britannica*, accessed October 4, 2019, https://www.britannica.com/topic/Mau-Mau.

6 Tom Barrett, "Tom Barrett Quotes," BrainyQuote, updated 2020, accessed December 1, 2020, https://www.brainyquote.com/quotes/tom_barrett_13243 7.

7 "Pop Culture Dictionary," Dictionary, updated 2020, accessed September 9, 2020, https://www.dictionary.com/e/pop-culture/cancel-culture/.

8 John Stossel, "Cancel Culture Is Out of Control," Reason, published July 8, 2020, accessed September 9, 2020, https://reason.com/2020/07/08/cancel-culture-is-out-of-control/.

9 "Karma in Hinduism," *Wikipedia,* last modified August 29, 2019, accessed September 1, 2019, https://en.wikipedia.org/wiki/Karma_in_Hinduism.

10 "As You Sow, So Shall You Reap," *Wiktionary,* last modified April 17, 2019, accessed September 1, 2019, https://en.wiktionary.org/wiki/as_you_sow,_so_shall_you_reap.

[11] Sakyong Mipham, "Sakyong Mipham Quotes," *AZ Quotes,* updated 2020, accessed December 1, 2020, https://www.azquotes.com/quote/538294.

[12] 10 Paul Coelho, *The Alchemist*, trans. Alan R. Clarke (San Francisco: Harper San Francisco, 1988), vii.

[13] Coelho, *The Alchemist*, x.

[14] Rabindranath Tagore, "Rabindranath Tagore Quotes," Goodreads, updated 2020, accessed December 1, 2020, https://www.goodreads.com/author/quotes/36913.Rabindranath_Tagor.

Sexual Abuse and Molestation

[15] American Psychological Association, "Sexual Abuse," *American Psychological Association*, updated 2019, accessed November 17, 2019, https://www.apa.org/topics/sexual-abuse/index.

[16] Wikipedia, "Sexual Abuse," *Wikipedia*, updated November 14, 2019, accessed November 17, 2019, https://en.wikipedia.org/wiki/Sexual_abuse.

[17] Mannat Mohanjeet Singh, Shradha S. Parsekar, and Sreekumaran, "An Epidemiological Overview of Child Sex Abuse," *Journal of Family Medicine and Primary Care* 3, no. 4 (Oct-Dec 2014): 430, accessed November 17, 2019,https://www.ncbi.nlm.nih.gov/pmc/articles/PMC4311357/
.

[18] Wikipedia, "Sexual Abuse."

[19] Wikipedia, "Sexual Abuse."

[20] Wikipedia, "Sexual Abuse."

Sexual Harassment

[21] Emily Crockett, "The History of Sexual Harassment Explains Why Many Women Wait So Long to Come Forward," *Vox*, published July 14, 2016, accessed November 17, 2019, https://www.vox.com/2016/7/14/12178412/roger-ailes-sexual-harassment-history-women-wait.

[22] Equal Employment Opportunity Commission, "Enforcement Efforts in the 1980s," *Equal Employment Opportunity Commission*, updated 2019, accessed November 20, 2019, https://www.eeoc.gov/eeoc/history/35th/1980s/enforcement.html.

23 National Conference of State Legislatures, "Sexual Harassment in the Workplace," *National Conference of State Legislatures,* updated March 28, 2019, accessed November 20, 2019, http://www.ncsl.org/research/labor-and-employment/sexual-harassment-in-the-workplace.aspx.

24 National Conference of State Legislatures, "Sexual Harassment in the Workplace."

25 Chicago Tribune, "#MeToo: A Timeline of Events," *Chicago Tribune*, published September 27, 2019, accessed November 23, 2019, https://www.chicagotribune.com/lifestyles/ct-me-too-timeline-20171208-htmlstory.html.

26 Chicago Tribune, "#MeToo: A Timeline of Events."

Childhood Abuse Continuing into Adulthood

27 Mayo Clinic, "Child Abuse," *Mayo Clinic*, updated 2019, accessed November 23, 2019, https://www.mayoclinic.org/diseases-conditions/child-abuse/symptoms-causes/syc-20370864.

28 Jonathan Lockwood Huie, "Forgive Others…," *Goodreads,* updated 2019, accessed November 23, 2019, https:// www.goodreads.com/quotes/4606206-forgive-others-

not-because-they-deserve-forgiveness-but-because-you.

[29] Author Unknown, "I forgive people…," *Daily Inspirational Quotes*, updated 2020, accessed December 1, 2020, https://www.dailyinspirationalquotes.in/2016/01/i-forgive-people.

[30] Author Unknown, "Do not judge people for the choices…," *Tiny Buddha*, updated 2020, accessed December 1, 2020, https://tinybuddha.com/wisdom-quotes/dont-judge-people-choices-make/.

[31] Author Unknown, "Never regret anything…," *Wisdom Quotes*, updated 2020, accessed December 1, 2020, https://www.wisdomquotes4u.com/never-regret-anything-that-has-happened-in-your-life/.

Recovery from Childhood Abuse

[32] Judith Lewis Herman, "In order to escape accountability…" *Goodreads*, updated 2019, accessed November 24, 2019, https://www.goodreads.com/quotes/tag/sexual-abuse.

[33] Medline Plus, "Conversion Disorder," *US Library of Medicine – Medline Plus*, updated November 6, 2019, accessed November 24, 2019, https://medlineplus.gov/ency/article/000954.htm

34 Shahid Ali, Shagufta Jabeen, Rebecca J. Pate, et al., "Conversion Disorder – Mind vs. Body: A Review,"*Innovations in Clinical Neuroscience 12*, no. 5-6 (May-June 2015): 27–33, published online May-Jun 2015, accessed November 24, 2019, https://www.ncbi.nlm.nih.gov/pmc/articles/PMC4479361/cited by/.

35 TR Nicholson, S. Aybek, T. Craig, et al., "Life Events and Escape in Conversion Disorder," *Psychological Medicine 46*, no. 12, (September 2016): 2617-2626, published online July 5, 2016, accessed November 24, 2019, https://www.ncbi.nlm.nih.gov/pubmed/27377290.

36 TR Nicholson, S. Aybek, T. Craig, et al., "Life Events and Escape in Conversion Disorder."

37Wikipedia, "Freud's Psychoanalytic Theories," *Wikipedia*, updated November 16, 2019, accessed November 24, 2019, https://en.wikipedia.org/wiki/Freud%27s_psychoanalytic_theor ies.

Sexual Abuse & Celebrities

38 Jessica Arnold, "Molly Ringwald Was Sexually Exploited When She Was 14 Years Old," *Sheknows*, published October 17, 2017, accessed November 26, 2019,

https://www.sheknows.com/entertainment/articles/1136629/molly-ringwald-op-ed-sexual-abuse-as-a-teenager/.

[39] Stephanie Zararek, Eliana Dockterman, and Haley Sweetland Edwards, "The Silence Breakers," *TIME,* published December 6, 2017, accessed November 26, 2019, https://time.com/time-person-of-the-year-2017-silence-breakers/.

[40] Stephanie Zararek, Eliana Dockterman, and Haley Sweetland Edwards, "The Silence Breakers."

[41] Ibid.

[42] Ibid.

[43] Author Unknown, "It is easy to judge…," *Daily Inspirational Quotes*, updated 2020, accessed December 1, 2020,https://www.dailyinspirationalquotes.in/2017/07/easy-judge-mistakes-others-difficult-recognize-mistakes/.

[44] Hilary Weaver, "Jennifer Lawrence's Harrowing Story Proves Hollywood's Sexual Harassment Goes Beyond Harvey Weinstein," *Vanity Fair*, published October 17, 2017, accessed November 26, 2019, https://www.vanityfair.com/style/2017/10/jennifer-lawrence-shares-story-of-sexual-assault-at-elle-women-in-hollywood.

45 Hilary Weaver, "Jennifer Lawrence's Harrowing Story Proves Hollywood's Sexual Harassment Goes Beyond Harvey Weinstein.

46 Samantha Conti, "Boston Globe Clarifies Karl Templar Did Not Sexually Coerce Models," *Boston Globe*, published October 19, 2018, accessed November 30, 2019, https://wwd.com/business-news/media/boston-globe-clarifies-karl-templer-did-not-sexually-coerce-models-1202887071/.

47 Philip Utz, "'All the Other Designers Hate Me'…Karl Lagerfeld Gets Ready to Tell All," *Numéro*, published April 12, 2018, accessed November 30, 2019, https://www.numero.com/en/fashion/interview-karl-lagerfeld-chanel-virgil-abloh-j-w-anderson-azzedine-alaia#_.

48 Philip Utz, "'All the Other Designers Hate Me'…Karl Lagerfeld Gets Ready to Tell All."

49 Monica Lewinsky, "Monica Lewinsky: Emerging from the 'House of Gaslight'"in the Age of #MeToo, *Vanity Fair*, published March 2018, accessed November 30, 2019, https://www.vanityfair.com/news/2018/02/monica- lewinsky-in-the-age-of-metoo.

50 Health Poverty Action, "Gender-Based Violence," *Health Poverty Action*, published 2018, accessed September 4,

2020 https://www.healthpovertyaction.org/how-poverty-is-created/women-girls/sexual-and-gender-based-violence/?

[51] Operation Underground Railroad, "We Exist to Rescue Children from Sex Trafficking," *Operation Underground Railroad*, updated 2018, accessed November 30, 2019, http://ourrescue.org/.

[52] Gul Tuysuz, "Turkish Women Rally Against Domestic Violence as Ruling Party Contemplates Leaving Key Rights Treaty." *CNN World*, updated August 5, 2020, accessed September 4, 2020, https://www.cnn.com/2020/08/05/europe/turkey-gender-protests-istanbul-convention-intl/index.html.

Sexual Abuse & Children

[53] Daisy Gonzalez-Diego, "M-DCPS Reinforces Highest Expectations of Professionalism, Accountability for Employee and Student Interactions," *Miami-Dade County Public Schools*, published February 13, 2019, accessed December 1, 2019, http://districtartifacts.dadeschools.net/Standard%203/3.11/District%20Professional%20Development%20Manual.pdf.

Sexual Abuse & Personal Responsibility

[54] Marguerite Ward and Rachel Premack, "What is a microaggression? 14 Things People Think Are Fine to Say at

Work – But Are Actually Racist, Sexist or Offensive," *Business Insider*, published July 24, 2020 accessed August 6, 2020, http://districtartifacts.dadeschools.net/Standard%203/3.11/Distr ict%20Professional%20Development%20Manual.pdf.

55 Candace Norcott PhD, "Q&A: Supporting Survivors of Childhood Sex Abuse," *University of Chicago Medicine*, published February 21, 2019, accessed December 6, 2019, https://www.uchicagomedicine.org/forefront/pediatrics-articles/2019/february/supporting-survivors-of-childhood-sexual-abuse.

The Catholic Church & Sex Abuse of Children

56 Laurie Goodstein and Sharon Otterman, "Catholic Priests Abused 1,000 Children in Pennsylvania, Report Says,"*The New York Times*, published August 14, 2018, accessed December 6, 2019, https://www.nytimes.com/2018/08/14/us/catholic-church-sex-abuse-pennsylvania.html.

57 Laurie Goodstein and Sharon Otterman, "Catholic Priests Abused 1,000 Children in Pennsylvania, Report Says."

58 Vanessa Romo and Sylvia Poggioli, "Pope Francis Expresses 'Shame and Sorrow' Over Pennsylvania Abuse Allegations," *NPR*, published August 16, 2018, accessed December 6, 2019, https://www.opb.org/news/article/npr-pope-

francis-expresses-shame-and-sorrow-over-latest-abuse-allegations/.

[59] Daniela Mohor, "In Chile, a Growing Shadow over the Church," *US News & World Report*, published June 5, 2018, accessed December 6, 2019, https://www.usnews.com/news/best-countries/articles/2018-06-05/abuse-scandals-erode-authority-of-catholic-church-in-chile.

[60] Daniela Mohor, "In Chile, a Growing Shadow over the Church."

[61] Wikipedia, "Catholic Church Sexual Abuse by Country," *Wikipedia*, updated December 9, 2019, accessed December 10, 2019, https://en.wikipedia.org/wiki/Catholic_Church_sexual_abuse_cases_by_country.

[62] Barbie Latza Nadeau, "The Secret Sex Lives of Nuns," *Daily Beast*, published May 15, 2019, accessed December 10, 2019, https://www.thedailybeast.com/the-secret-sex-lives-of-nuns.

[63] Barbie Latza Nadeau, "The Secret Sex Lives of Nuns."

⁶⁴ Tom Corrigan "Catholic Church Used Bankruptcy for Sexual-Assault Cases. Now Others Are Following Suit." *The Wall Street Journal*, published December 27, 2018, accessed December 10, 2019, https://www.wsj.com/articles/ catholic-church-used-bankruptcy-for-sexual-assault-cases-now-others-are-following-suit-11545906600.

⁶⁵ Linda Givetash and Reuters, "In Visit to Transformed Ireland, Pope Says He Shares Outrage over Sex Abuse Scandals," *NBC News*, published August 25, 2018, accessed December 2019 ,https://www.nbcnews.com/news/religion/pope-francis-arrives-transformed-ireland-abuse-crises-rage-n903831.

⁶⁶ The Wealth Record, "Catholic Church Net Worth," *The Wealth Record*, published June 2, 2019, accessed December 10, 2019, https://www.thewealthrecord.com/celebs-bio-wiki-salary-earnings-2019-2020-2021-2022-2023-2024-2025/other/catholic-church-net-worth/.

University Athletes & Sexual Abuse

⁶⁷ Chris Morris, "Six Women Sue USC for Alleged Sexual Misconduct by Campus Gynecologist," *Fortune*, published May 22, 2018, accessed December 12, 2019, https://fortune.com/2018/05/22/usc-gynecologist-sexual-assault/.

[68] Anna Sturla and Eliott C. McLaughlin, "Super Bowl Champ Among the Latest Wave of Athletes Accusing Michigan Wolverines' Doctor of Abuse," *CNN*, updated August 12, 2020, accessed August 15, 2020, https://www.cnn.com/2020/08/12/us/university-michigan-dr-robert-anderson-allegations-sex-abuse/index.html.

[69] Eric Levenson, "Larry Nasser Sentenced up to 175 Years in Prison for Decades of Sexual Abuse," *CNN*, published January 24, 2018, accessed December 12, 2019, https://www.cnn.com/2018/01/24/us/larry-nassar-sentencing/index.html.

[70] Eric Levenson, "Larry Nasser Sentenced up to 175 Years in Prison for Decades of Sexual Abuse," *CNN*, published January 24, 2018, accessed December 12, 2019, https://www.cnn.com/2018/01/24/us/larry-nassar-sentencing/index.html.

[71] Dwight Adams, "Victims Share What Larry Nasser Did to Them Under the Guise of Medical Treatment," *IndyStar*, published January 25, 2018, accessed December 12, 2019, https://www.indystar.com/story/news/ 2018/01/25/heres-what-larry-nassar-actually-did-his-patients/1065165001/.

[72] Mitch Smith and Ademona Hartocollis, "Michigan State's $500 Million for Nassar's Victims Dwarfs Other

Settlements," *The New York Times*, published May 16, 2018, accessed December 12, 2019, https://www.nytimes.com/2018/05/16/us/larry-nassar-michigan-state-settlement.html.

Olympic Gymnasts and Abuse

[73] The Straits Times, "Gymnastics: The Karolyi Ranch Seen as Ground Zero for Larry Nasser's Reign of Terror," *The Straits Times*, published January 20, 2018, accessed December 12, 2019, https://www.straitstimes.com/sport/ gymnastics-the-karolyi-ranch-seen-as-ground-zero-for-larry-nassars-reign-of-terror.

[74] John Cazarez and Tony Marco, "Lawyer Claims Karolyi's Are Lying in Their Lawsuit Against USA Gymnastics and USOC," *CNN*, published May 4, 2018, accessed December 12, 2019, https://www.cnn.com/2018/05/04/us/martha-karolyi-lawsuit-date-discrepancy/index.html.

[75] Meghan O'Rouke, "Why Extreme Gymnastics Will Dominate the Rio Olympics," *The Atlantic*, published July/August 2016, accessed December 12, 2019, https://www.theatlantic.com/magazine/archive/2016/07/why-extreme-gymnastics-will-dominate-the-rio-olympics/485582/.

[76] Holly Yan, "USA Gymnastics Files for Bankruptcy

after Hefty Lawsuits over Larry Nasser," *CNN*, published December 5, 2018, accessed December 12, 2019, https://www.cnn.com/2018/12/05/us/usa-gymnastics-files-for-bankruptcy/index.html.

[77] Holly Yan, "USA Gymnastics Files for Bankruptcy after Hefty Lawsuits over Larry Nasser."

[78] Author Unknown, "Change comes from constructive thought…," *Brahmakumaris Online Learning*, updated 2020, accessed December 1, 2020, https://www.facebook.com/brahmakumaris.onlinelearning/posts/thought-for-today/894586041369998/.

Identity and Gender Autonomy

[79] Kris Gage, "How the Women's Conversation Isn't Helping," *Medium*, published April 22, 2018, accessed December 14, 2019, https://medium.com/@krisgage/how-the-womens-conversation-hurts-women-52e385b4afbe.

[80] Kris Gage, "How the Women's Conversation Isn't Helping."

[81] Mark Manson, "What's the Point of Self-improvement Anyway?" *MarkManson*, published July 20, 2017, accessed December 16, 2019, https://markmanson.net/self-improvement.

[82] Eleanor Roosevelt, "In the Long Run, We Shape Out Lives...," *BrainyQuote*, updated 2019, accessed December 16, 2019 https://www.brainyquote.com/quotes/eleanor_roosevelt_121109.

#MeToo Movement

[83] Sandra Garcia, "The Woman Who Created #MeToo Long before Hashtags," *The New York Times*, published October 20, 2019, accessed December 15, 2019, https://www.nytimes.com/2017/10/20/us/me-too-movement-tarana-burke.html.

[84] Dalvin Brown, "19 Million Tweets Later: A Look at #MeToo a Year after the Hashtag Went Viral," *USA Today*, published October 13, 2018, accessed December 15, 2019, https://www.usatoday.com/story/news/2018/10/13/metoo-impact-hashtag-made-online/1633570002/.

[85] Sandra Garcia, "The Woman Who Created #MeToo Long before Hashtags."

[86] Anna Codrea-Rado, "#MeToo Floods Social Media with Stories of Harassment and Assault," *The New York Times*, published October 16, 2017, accessed December 15, 2019,

https://www.nytimes.com/2017/10/16/technology/metoo-twitter-facebook.html.

[87] Anna North, "263 Celebrities, Politicians, CEOs, and Others Who Have Been Accused of Sexual Misconduct since April 2017," *Vox*, published January 9, 2019, accessed December 15, 2019, https://www.vox.com/a/sexual-harassment-assault-allegations-list.

[88] West's Encyclopedia of American Law, "Reasonable Doubt," *West's Encyclopedia of American Law*, updated 2006, accessed December 17, 2019, https://legal dictionary.thefreedictionary.com/reasonable+doubt.

[89] Professor Douglas O. Linder, "The Stained Blue Dress that Almost Lost a Presidency," *Famous Trials*, updated 2019, accessed December 17, 2019, https://www.famous-trials.com/clinton/889-lewinskydress.

[90] Dr. Grant Hilary Brenner MD, FAPA, "Why Do Certain Men Resort to Sexual Harassment?," *Psychology Today*, published July 16, 2018, accessed December 17, 2019, https://www.psychologytoday.com/us/blog/experimentations/201807/why-do-certain-men-resort-sexual-harassment.

[91] Editors of Encyclopedia Britannica, "Hippie Subculture," *Encyclopedia Britannica*, updated 2019, accessed

December 18, 2019, https://www.britannica.com/topic/Pan-Arabism.

92 Wikipedia, "Sexual Revolution in the 60s, United States," *Wikipedia*, updated September 29, 2019, accessed December 18, 2019, https://en.wikipedia.org/wiki/Sexual_revolution_in_1960s_United_States.

93 RAINN, "Criminal Statutes of Limitations New York," *RAINN*, updated December 2017, accessed December 18, 2019, https://apps.rainn.org/policy/policy-crime definitions.

94 Rachel Farrow, "See the Net Worth of Stormy Daniels, Adult Film Star," Yahoo! Finance, published April 26, 2018, accessed December 18, 2019, https://finance.yahoo.com/news/see-net-worth-stormy-daniels-230024190.html.

95 Erik Moshe, "An Interview with Historian Nikki Taylor," George Washington University: History News Network, published February 16, 2019, accessed December 18, 2019, https://historynewsnetwork.org/article/171036.

96 Tom Kludt, "How Fox News Broke the Bill O'Reilly Story to Its Viewers," CNN Business, published April 20, 2017,

accessed December 18, 2019,
https://money.cnn.com/2017/04/19/media/fox-news-covers-bill-oreilly/index.html.

[97] Michelle Castillo, "How Much Money Did O'Reilly Bring in for Fox?," CNBC News, published April 20, 2017, accessed December 18, 2019, https://www.nbcnews.com/business/business-news/how-much-money-did-o-reilly-bring-fox-n748756.

[98] Wikipedia, "Bill O'Reilly, Political Commentator," Wikipedia, updated December 18, 2019, accessed December 18, 2019, https://en.wikipedia.org/wiki/Bill_O%27Reilly_(political_commentator).

[99] Wikipedia, "Bill O'Reilly, Political Commentator," Wikipedia, updated December 18, 2019, accessed December 18, 2019, https://en.wikipedia.org/wiki/Bill_O%27Reilly_(political_commentator).

[100] U.S. Census Bureau, "Child Stats: Structure and Children's Living Arrangements" Child Stats, published 2012, updated annually, accessed August 3, 2020,https://www.childstats.gov/americaschildren/tables/fam1a.asp.

[101] Editorial Board, "The Cosby Survivors Finally Get Justice, but Think About Those Hurt Along the Way," The Washington Post, published April 27, 2018, accessed December 19, 2019, https://www.washingtonpost.com/ opinions/the-cosby-survivors-finally-get-justice-but-think-of-those-hurt-along-the-way/.

[102] Meredith Mandell, Adam Reiss, and Daniella Silva, "Bill Cosby Found Guilty of Assault in Retrial," NBC News, published April 26, 2018, accessed December 19, 2019, https://www.nbcnews.com/storyline/bill-cosby-scandal/bill-cosby-found-guilty-sexual-assault-retrial-n869121.

[103] Emily Shugerman, "Five Universities Revoke Bill Cosby's Honorary Degrees After Sexual Assault Conviction,"Independent, published April 28, 2019, accessed December 19, 2019, https://www.independent.co.uk/news/world/ americas/bill-cosby-convicted-sexual-assault-honorary-degrees-revoked-temple-university-a8326491.html.

[104] Katia Hetter, "Bill Cosby Resigns from Temple University Board," CNN, published December 2, 2014, accessed December 19, 2019, https://www.cnn.com/2014/12/01/showbiz/bill-cosby-resigns-temple-university-board/index.html.

[105] Jennifer Konerman and Gregg Kilday, "Roman Polanski, Bill Cosby Booted from Film Academy," Hollywood Reporter, published May 3, 2018, accessed December 19, 2019, https://www.hollywoodreporter.com/news/roman-polanski-bill-cosby-booted-academy-1108390.

[106] Maria Vultaggio, "Who is Timothy Heller? About Melanie Martinez Rape Accuser," *Newsweek*, published December 5, 2017, accessed December 19, 2019, https://www.newsweek.com/melanie-martinez-timothy-heller-rape-735686.

[107] Aaron Feis, "Asia Argento Accused of Paying Hush Money to Silence Sexual Assault Allegations," PageSix, published August 19, 2018, accessed December 28, 2019, https://pagesix.com/2018/08/19/asia-argento-accused-of-paying-hush-money-to-silence-sexual-assault-allegations/.

[108] Jamie Ross, "Report; Asia Argento Confesses to Having Sex with Underage Teen in Leaked Text Messages,"Daily Beast, published August 22, 2018, accessed December 28, 2019, https://www.thedailybeast.com/report-asia- argento-confesses-to-having-sex-with-underage-teen-in-leaked-text-messages.

[109] BBC News, "Harvey Weinstein Scandal: Who Has Accused Him of What?," BBC News, published January 10,

2019, accessed December 28, 2019,
https://www.bbc.com/news/entertainment-arts-41580010.

[110] Alesandra Dubin, "Asia Argento Claims Anthony
Bourdain Paid Off Her Accuser," BravoTV, published August
21, 2018, accessed December 28, 2019,
https://www.bravotv.com/the-feast/asia-argento-claims-
anthony-bourdain-paid-off-sexual-assault-accuser-jimmy-
bennett.

[111] Eliana Dockterman, "What to Know About the Casey
Affleck Oscar Controversy," Time, published January 25, 2017,
accessed December 28, 2019,
https://www.yahoo.com/news/know-casey-affleck-oscar-
controversy-213025429.html.

[112] Eliana Dockterman, "What to Know About the Casey
Affleck Oscar Controversy."

[113] Ben Child, "Casey Affleck Settles Sexual Harassment
Lawsuits," The Guardian, published September 15, 2010,
accessed December 28, 2019,
https://www.theguardian.com/film/2010/sep/15/casey-affleck-
settles-harassment-lawsuits.

[114] HG.org Legal Resources, "Different Standards of
Proof," HG.Legal Resources, updated 2019, accessed

December 31, 2019, https://www.hg.org/legal-articles/different-standards-of-proof-6363.

[115] Aaron Katersky, "Former Aspiring Actor Claims Harvey Weinstein Sexually Assaulted Her at 16: Lawsuit," ABC News, published December 19, 2019, accessed December 31, 2019, https://abcnews.go.com/Entertainment/aspiring-actor-claims-harvey-weinstein-sexually-assaulted-16/story?id=67834181.

[116] Erik Ortiz and Corky Siemaszko, "NBC Fires Matt Lauer after Sexual Misconduct Review," NBC News, published November 29, 2017, accessed December 31, 2019, https://www.nbcnews.com/storyline/sexual-misconduct/nbc-news-fires-today-anchor-matt-lauer-after-sexual-misconduct-n824831.

[117] Erik Ortiz and Corky Siemaszko, "NBC Fires Matt Lauer after Sexual Misconduct Review."

[118] Elizabeth Wagmeister and Ramin Setoodeh, "Tom Brokaw Accused of Sexual Harassment by Former NBC Anchor," Variety, published April 26, 2018, accessed December 31, 2019, https://variety.com/2018/tv/news/tom-brokaw-sexual-harassment-nbc-news-correspondent-1202789627/.

[119] Daniel Kreps, "Rachel Maddow, Maria Shriver Sign Letter Defending Tom Brokaw," Rolling Stone, published April 28, 2018, accessed December 31, 2019, https://www.rollingstone.com/tv/tv-news/rachel-maddow-maria-shriver-sign-letter-defending-tom-brokaw-628136/.

[120] Dr. Alex Lickerman, M.D., "The Value of a Good Reputation," Psychology Today, published April 22, 2010, accessed December 31, 2019, https://www.psychologytoday.com/us/blog/happiness-in-world/201004/the-value-good-reputation.

[121] William Congreve, "Hell Has No Fury Like a Woman Scorned," Phrases, updated 2019, accessed January 2, 2020, https://www.phrases.org.uk/meanings/hell-has-no-fury-like-a-woman-scorned.html.

[122] Wikipedia, "Joe Paterno," Wikipedia, updated January 2, 2020, accessed January 2, 2020, https://en.wikipedia.org/wiki/Joe Paterno.

[123] Realreporting.org/NewsLanc.com, "Summary of King & Spalding Findings: Injustice Regarding Joe Paterno," *Realreporting.org/NewsLanc*, published February 10, 2013, accessed January 2, 2020, https://newslanc.com/ summary-of-king-spalding-findings-injustice-regarding-joe-paterno/.

124 Phrases.org, "Don't Throw the Baby Out with the Bathwater," *Phrases*, updated 2019, accessed January 2, 2020, https://www.phrases.org.uk/meanings/dont-throw-the-baby-out-with-the-bathwater.html.

125 Biography.org, "The Rise and Fall of Joe Paterno," *Biography*, updated 2019, accessed January 2, 2020, https://www.biography.com/news/joe-paterno-movie-hbo-paterno.

126 ESPN.com, "Joe Paterno Is Now Winningest Coach," *ESPN*, published January 16, 2015, accessed January 2, 2020, https://www.espn.com/college-football/story/_/id/12179571/joe-paterno-111-wins-were-vacated-restored.

127 Gordon S. White Jr., "Paterno Spurns Patriots and $1.3-Million Contract," *New York Times*, published January 7, 1973, accessed January 2, 2020, https://www.nytimes.com/1973/01/07/archives/paterno-spurns-patriots-and-13million-contract-paterno-rejects.html.

128 Wikipedia, "Jerry Sandusky," *Wikipedia*, updated December 27, 2019, accessed January 3, 2020, https:// en.wikipedia.org/wiki/Jerry Sandusky.

129 Jane Mayer, "The Case of Al Franken," *The New Yorker*, published July 22, 2019, accessed January 3, 2020, https://www.newyorker.com/magazine/2019/07/29/the-case-of-al-franken.

130 Jane Mayer, "The Case of Al Franken."

131 Justin Baragona, "Mediaite's John Ziegler Defends Al Franken in Fiery HLN Debate: We've Lost Our Minds," *Mediaite*, published November 17, 2017, accessed January 3, 2020, https://www.mediaite.com/tv/mediaites-john- ziegler-defends-al-franken-in-fiery-hln-debate-weve-lost-our-minds/.

132 Adam Edelman and Leigh Ann Caldwell, "Saturday Night Live Women Defend Al Franken After Groping Allegations," *NBC News*, published November 21, 2017, accessed January 3, 2020, https://www.nbcnews.com/politics/politics-news/saturday-night-live-women-defend-franken-after-groping-allegations-n822806.

133 Daniella Diaz, "Sen. Amy Klobuchar on Not Denouncing Franken: I Felt I Was in a Different Role," *CNN Politics*, published December 8, 2017, accessed January 3, 2020, https://www.cnn.com/2017/12/08/politics/amy-klobuchar-senate-al-franken-minnesota/index.html.

[134] Lisa Lerer and Shane Goldmacher, "Al Franken Has Regrets. Kristian Gillibrand Does Not." *New York Times*, published July 23, 2019, accessed January 4, 2020, https://www.nytimes.com/2019/07/23/us/politics/al-franken-kirsten-gillibrand.html.

[135] Terry Gross, "Journalist Jane Mayer on the Many Mysteries in the Accusations Against Al Franken," *WPRL*, published July 26, 2019, accessed January 3, 2020, https://www.wprl.org/post/journalist-jane-mayer-many-mysteries-accusations-against-al-franken.

[136] Elizabeth Loftus, "Elizabeth Loftus Quotes," *AZ Quotes*, updated 2020, accessed December 1, 2020, https://www.azquotes.com/author/50272-Elizabeth_Loftus#:%.

Historical Perspective

[137] Russell Grigg, "Eve Created from Adam's Rib," *Creation*, published online October 2013,(Creation35(4): 42-44), accessed February 11, 2020, https://creation.com/eve-adams-rib.

[138] Russell Grigg, "To Defame the Character of God," *Creation,* published online June 1994, (Creation16(3): 48-49),

accessed February 11, 2020, https://creation.com/strategy-of-the-devil.

139 Lisa Hartz Rump, "Is Christianity Oppressive to Women?," *Christianity Today*, published February 8, 2008, accessed February 11, 2020, https://www.christianitytoday.com/history/2008/august/is-christianity-oppressive-to-women.html.

140 Wikipedia, "Trinitarianism in the Church Fathers," *Wikipedia*, updated December 2, 2019, accessed February 11, 2020, https://en.wikipedia.org/wiki/Trinitarianism_in_the_Church_Fathers.

141 Wikipedia, "Women in the Patristic Age," *Wikipedia*, updated December 17, 2019, accessed February 11, 2020, https://en.wikipedia.org/wiki/Women_in_the_patristic_age.

142 Tertullian, "Works of Tertullian," *Tertullian*, updated December 10, 1999, accessed February 11, 2020, http://www.tertullian.org/works.htm.

143 Mathew V. Brown,"The 'Woman' of Augustine of Hippo,*"Priscilla Papers: The Academic Journal of CBE International 4*, No.4 (1990) 10-11, accessed February 15, 2020,

https://www.cbeinternational.org/sites/default/files/hippo.pdf.

[144] Wikipedia, "Augustine of Hippo," *Wikipedia*, updated February 14, 2020, accessed February 15, 2020, https://en.wikipedia.org/wiki/Augustine_of_Hippo#Original_si n.

[145] Augustine, "Political Writings," ed. Ernest L. Fortin, Roland Gunn, and Douglas Kries, (Indianapolis: Hackett Publishing Co., 1994), 252, ebook, https://books.google.com/books?e.

[146] Wikipedia, "Persecution of Christians in the Roman Empire, *Wikipedia*, updated February 10, 2020, accessed February 15, 2020, https://en.wikipedia.org/wiki/Persecution_of_Christians_in_the _Roman_Empire.

[147] Dan Lamothe, 'The U.S. Military's Long Uncomfortable History with Prostitution, *Washington Post*, published October 31, 2014, accessed August 4, 2020, https://www.washingtonpost.com/news/checkpoint/wp/2014/10 /31/the-u-s-militarys-long-uncomfortable-history-with-prostitution-gets-new-attention/.

[148] Cultural India, "Raja Ram Mohan Roy," *Cultural India*, updated 2020, accessed February 18, 2020, https://

www.culturalindia.net/reformers/raja-ram-mohan-roy.html.

149 Cultural India, "Raja Ram Mohan Roy."

150 Wikipedia, "Ram Mohan Roy," *Wikipedia*, updated January 28, 2020, accessed February 18, 2020, https://en.wikipedia.org/wiki/Ram_Mohan_Roy.

151 Wikipedia, "Female Infanticide," *Wikipedia*, updated January 7, 2020, accessed February 18, 2020, https://en.wikipedia.org/wiki/Female_infanticide.

152 Wikipedia, "Female Infanticide."

153 Genetics, the Tech@Stanford University, "Chromosomes," *Genetics, the Tech*, updated April 5, 20212, accessed February 18, 2020, https://genetics.thetech.org/ask-a-geneticist/which-parent-decides-whether-baby-will- be-boy-or-girl.

154 Kritika Sharma, "Number of Women Enrolling in Higher Education Rises 1,350% in Seven Years,"*The Print India*, published July 27, 2018, accessed February 21, 2020, https://theprint.in/india/governance/number- of-women-enrolling-in-higher-education-rises-1350-per-cent-in-7-years/89453.

155 Consultancy.asia, "Economic Boom Will See 500 Million Indians Enter the Middle Class within a Decade," *Consultancy.asia*, published April 18, 2019, accessed February 21, 2020, https://www.consultancy.asia/news/2144/ economic-boom-will-see-500-million-indians-enter-middle-class-within-a-decade.

156 Consultancy.asia, "Economic Boom Will See 500 Million Indians Enter the Middle Class within a Decade."

157 Jim Chappelow, "Gross Domestic Product (GDP)," *Investopedia*, updated June 27, 2019, accessed February 21, 2020, https://www.investopedia.com/terms/g/gdp.asp.

158 Neetu Chandra Sharma, "Non-marriage Very Rare in India but Divorces Doubled in Past Two Decades, *Live Mint*, published June 25, 2019, accessed February 21, 2020, https://www.livemint.com/.

159 Wikipedia, "One-child Policy," *Wikipedia*, updated February 17, 2020, accessed February 22, 2020, https:// en.wikipedia.org/wiki/One-child_policy.

160 Kallie Szczepanski, "Female Infanticide in Asia," *Thought*, updated December 9, 2019, accessed February 22, 2020, https://www.thoughtco.com/female-infanticide-in-asia-195450.

161 Statista Research Department, "Population in China 2008 – 2018, by Gender," *Statista*, published February 18, 2020, accessed February 22, 2020, https://www.statista.com/statistics/263765/total-population-of-china/.

162 Roseann Lake, "China, A Wife Less Ordinary," *1843 Magazine*, published April/May 2018, accessed February 22, 2020, https://www.1843magazine.com/features/a-wife-less-ordinary.

163 Roseann Lake, "China, A Wife Less Ordinary."

164 Wei Lee, Commentary: Vietnamese Brides Increasingly the Choice for China's Bachelors," *Channel News Asia*, published January 18, 2020, accessed February 22, 2020, https://www.channelnewsasia.com/news/commentary/vietnamese-brides-for-single-men-in-china-marriage-brokers-12271868.

165 Li Mo, "Trends in Divorce Rate and Its Regional Disparity in China," *Journal of Comparative Studies 48 (4): 383*, University of Sociology, University of Calgary, 2017.

166 Xinhua News Agency, "China Sees Over Nine Million Marriages Last Year," *Gale General One File*, published January 19, 2020, accessed February 24, 2020,

https://link-gale
com.db04.linccweb.org/apps/doc/A611702415/.

[167] Christiane Amanpour, "Sex and Love around the World," *Netflix*, broadcast 2018, accessed February 25, 2020, https://www.netflix.com/title/81011682.

[168] Robin Harding, "Birth Rates in Japan Fall to Lowest Level on Record," *The Irish Times*, published December 22, 2017, accessed February 25, 2020, https://www.irishtimes.com/news/world/asia-pacific/birth-rates-in-japan-fall-to-lowest-level-on-record-1.3336732.

[169] Robin Harding, "Birth Rates in Japan Fall to Lowest Level on Record."

[170] ThoughtCo., "Story of the Comfort Women of World War II," *Thought Co.*, updated January 20, 2020, accessed February 25, 2020, https://www.thoughtco.com/world-war-ii-comfort-women-3530682.

[171] James C. Thompson, "Women in Ancient Egypt," *Women in the Ancient World*, published July 2010, accessed March 7, 2020, http://www.womenintheancientworld.com/women_in_ancient_egypt.htm.

172 James C. Thompson, "Women in Ancient Egypt."

173 Radwa Khalil, Ahmed A. Moustafa, Marie Z. Moftah, and Ahmed A. Karim, "How Knowledge of Ancient Egyptian Women Can Influence Today's Gender Role: Does History Matter in Gender Psychology?," *Frontier Psychology*, published January 5, 2017, accessed March 13, 2020, https://www.frontiersin.org/articles/10.3389/fpsyg.2016.02053/full.

174 Radwa Khalil, Ahmed A. Moustafa, Marie Z. Moftah, and Ahmed A. Karim, "How Knowledge of Ancient Egyptian Women Can Influence Today's Gender Role: Does History Matter in Gender Psychology?"

175 Wikipedia, "Gender Inequality in Egypt," *Wikipedia*, updated January 11, 2020, accessed March 13, 2020, https://en.wikipedia.org/wiki/Gender_inequality_in_Egypt#Employment.

176 Basil El-Dabh, "99.3% of Egyptian Women Experienced Sexual Harassment: Report," *Daily News Egypt*, published April 28, 2013, accessed March 13, 2020, https://wwww.dailynewssegypt.com/2013/04/28/99-3-of-egyptian-women-experienced-sexual-harassment-report/.

177 Wikipedia, "Mass Sexual Assault in Egypt,"

Wikipedia, updated February 21, 2020, accessed March 13, 2020, https://en.wikipedia.org/wiki/Mass_sexual_assault_in_Egypt.

[178] Women's International League for Peace and Freedom, "Egypt: Worst Place in the Middle East to Be a Woman," *WILPF*, published January 8, 2014, accessed March 13, 2020, https://www.wilpf.org/egypt-worst-place-in-the-middle-east-to-be-a-woman.

[179] Sanja Kelly, "Women's Rights in the Middle East and North Africa: Recent Gains and New Opportunities for Women's Rights in the Gulf Arab States," *Freedom House*, published July 16, 2010, accessed August 5, 2020, https://freedomhouse.org/sites/default/files/Women's%20Rights%20in%20the%20Middle%20East%20and%20Noth%20Africa,%20Gulf%20Edition.pdf.

[180] Past Factory, "The Real Truth Behind the Viking Culture," *Past Factory*, updated 2020, accessed March 19, 2020, https://www.pastfactory.com/history/the-real-truth-behind-the-viking-culture/2/?chrome=1.

[181] Shawn M. Carter, "The Gender Pay Gap is Still 20%--but Millennial Women Are Closing in on Men," *CNBC*, published August 7, 2017, accessed March 19, 2020, https://www.cnbc.com/2017/08/07/gender-pay-gap-is-still-20-

percent-but-millennial-women-are-closing-in.html#:~:text=Money.

[182] Joe Vito Moubry, "It's Time to Change the Masculine Model," Volante Online, published April 18, 2018, accessed March 19, 2020, http://volanteonline.com/2018/04/its-time-to-change-the-masculinity-model/.

[183] Nick Duffell, "The Impact of Hyper-rationality on Men's Hearts and the Way Out," Medium, published May 6, 2017, accessed March 19, 2020, https://medium.com/perspectiva-institute/the-impact-of-hyper-rationality-on-mens-hearts-and-the-way-out-1bf6baf56e51.

[184] E. L. James, Fifty Shades of Grey, (New York: Vintage Books, 2011), Introduction.

[185] Sheryl Sandberg, *Lean In*, (London: Penguin Random House, 2015), 104-121.

[186] Sandberg, *Lean In*, 122-140.

[187] Ibid, Page 115.

[188] Ibid, Page 130.

The Yin and the Yang

189 Penelope Rodriguez, "The Yin and Yang of Masculine and Feminine," *Mind Key*, published August 18, 2017, accessed March 30, 2020, http://mindkey.me/yin-yang-masculine-feminine/.

190 U.S. Department of Labor, "Women's Bureau: History, An Overview 1920 – 2020," *DOL*, updated 2020, accessed March 30, 2020, https://www.dol.gov/agencies/wb/about/history.

191 Susan Stamberg, "Female World War II Pilots: The Original Fly Girls," *NPR*, published March 9, 2010, accessed March 30, 2020, https://www.npr.org/2010/03/09/123773525/female-wwii-pilots-the-original-fly-girls.

192 Elizabeth Jacobs and Kate Bahn, "Women's History Month: U.S. Women's Labor Force Participation,"*Equitable Growth*, published March 22, 2019, accessed April 4, 2020, https://equitablegrowth.org/womens- history-month-u-s-womens-labor-force-participation/.

193 Jack Rosenthal, "Women Made Two-Thirds of Gain s of Jobs in 1960's," *New York Times*, published February 12, 1973, accessed April 4, 2020,

https://www.nytimes.com/1973/02/12/archives/women-made-twothirds-of-gains-of-jobs-in-1960s-nomenclature-a.html.

194 Catalyst, "Women in the Work Force – United States: Quick Take," *Catalyst*, published June 5, 2019, accessed April 4, 2020, https://www.catalyst.org/research/women-in-the-workforce-united-states/.

195 Bryce Covert, "The Best Era for Working Women Was Twenty Years Ago," *New York Times*, published September 2, 2017, accessed April 4, 2020, https://www.nytimes.com/2017/01/24/business/economy/women-labor-force.html.

196 Sandberg, *Lean In*, Page 152.

197 Kathy Kurchiek, "Availability, Use of Paternity Leave Remains Rare in the United States," *SHRM*, published August 16, 2019, accessed April 4, 2020, https://www.shrm.org/resourcesandtools/hr-topics/behavioral-competencies/global-and-cultural-effectiveness/pages/availability-use-of-paternity-leave-remains-rare-in-us.aspx.

198 U.S. Equal Employment Opportunity Commission, "Overview: Authority and Role," *EEOC*, updated 2020, accessed April 4, 2020, https://www.eeoc.gov/eeoc/.

199 Gary Sheftick, "Army Offers More Flexibility with New Parental leave Policy," *Army*, published January 31, 2019, accessed April 4, 2020, https://www.army.mil/article/216774/army_offers_more_flexibility_with_new_parental_leave_policy.

200 Britni de la Cretaz, "Joe Biden Faces Sexual Allegations from a Former Staffer," *Yahoo*, published March 27, 2020, accessed April 9, 2020, https://www.yahoo.com/lifestyle/joe-biden-faces-sexual-assault-181441242.html.

201 Samantha Delbick, "#MeToo: Better for Business," *Law for Business USC*, published November 28, 2018, accessed April 9, 2020, http://lawforbusiness.usc.edu/metoo-better-for-business/.

202 Eric Baculinao, "China Tackles Masculinity Crisis, Tries to Stop 'Effeminate' Boys," *NBC News*, published January 9, 2017, accessed April 9, 2020, https://www.nbcnews.com/news/china/china-tackles-masculinity-crisis-tries-stop-effeminate-boys-n703461.

203 Charlie Morton, "The Unwanted Women of China," *International Love Scout*, published June 3, 2019, accessed April 9, 2020, https://www.internationallovescout.com/the-truth/sheng-nu-the-unwanted-women-of-china.

[204] Mandy Len Catron, "What You Lose When You Gain a Spouse," *The Atlantic*, published July 2, 2019, accessed April 9, 2020, https://www.theatlantic.com/family/archive/2019/07/case-against-marriage/591973/.

[205] A.W. Geiger and Gretchen Livingston, "8 Facts about Love and Marriage in America," *Pew Research*, published February 13, 2019, accessed April 9, 2020, https://www.pewresearch.org/fact-tank/2019/02/13/8-facts-about-love-and-marriage/.

[206] Kate Julian, "Why Are Young People Having So Little Sex?," *The Atlantic,* published December 2018, accessed April 9, 2020, https://www.theatlantic.com/magazine/archive/2018/12/the-sex-recession/573949/.

[207] Roland Kelts, "Japan Leads the Way in Sexless Love," *The Guardian*, published December 27, 2011, accessed April 9, 2020, https://www.theguardian.com/commentisfree/2011/dec/27/japan-men-sexless-love.

[208] Prince Ea, "Cute Quotes," *Pinterest*, updated 2020, accessed April 9, 2020, https://www.pinterest.com/pin/557039047641859648.

[209] Judith Newman, "'Lean In': Five years Later," *New York Times*, published March 16, 2018, accessed April 10, 2020, https://www.nytimes.com/2018/03/16/business/lean-in-five-years-later.html.

[210] The World News, "'Lean In' Five Years Later, - Don't Let History of Gender Define…," *The World News*, published March 16, 2018, accessed December 1, 2020,https://theworldnews.net/us-news/lean-in-five-years-later.

[211] Lorraine Bracco, "You Can't Change Other People. You Can Only Change Yourself." *Goodreads*, updated March 28, 2020, accessed May 24, 2020, https://www.goodreads.com/quotes/115708-you-can-t-change-other-people-you- can-only-change-yourself.

Roles of Men and Women in the Workplace

[212] Heather Mac Donald, "The Negative Impact of the #MeToo Movement," *Imprimis, Hillsdale College,"* 47, No.4, (April 2018), accessed April 10, 2020, https://imprimis.hillsdale.edu/the-negative-impact-of-the-metoo-movement/.

[213] Clare Cain Miller, "Even Among Harvard Graduates, Women Fall Short of Their Work Expectations," *New York Times*, published November 28, 2014, accessed April 10, 2020,

https://www.nytimes.com/2014/11/30/ upshot/even-among-harvard-graduates-women-fall-short-of-their-work-expectations.html.

[214] Sandberg, *Lean In*, Page 99.

[215] Sandberg, *Lean In*, Page 103.

[216] Ross Chainey, "What Just Happened? The Biggest Stories from Davos 2018," *We Forum*, published January 26, 2018, accessed April 10, 2020, https://www.weforum.org/agenda/2018/01/davos-2018-biggest-stories/.

[217] Timothy B. Lee, "Google Fires Engineer Who Crossed the Line with Diversity Memo," *Arstechnica*, published August 7, 2017, accessed April 10, 2020, https://arstechnica.com/tech-policy/2017/08/google-fires-engineer-who-crossed-the-line-with-diversity-memo/.

[218] Jonathan Spicer and Ann Saphir, "New York Fed Chief Selection Process Draws Fire from Politicians,"*Reuters*, published March 28, 2018, accessed April 10, 2020, https://www.reuters.com/article/us-usa-fed-new- york/new-york-fed-chief-selection-process-draws-fire-from-politicians-idUSKBN1H43HD.

[219] Business Wire, "30% Club Launches in the United States," *Business Wire*, published April 29, 2014, accessed April 10, 2020, https://www.businesswire.com/news/home/20140429006376/en/30-Club-Launches-United-States.

[220] Harvard Law School Forum, "Gender Parity on Boards Around the World," *Harvard Law School on Corporate Governance*, published January 5, 2017, accessed July 21, 2020, https://corpgov.law.harvard.edu/2017/01/05/gender-parity-on-boards-around-the-world/.

[221] Ibid.

[222] Marguerite Ward and Rachel Premack, "What is a microaggression? 14 Things People Think Are Fine to Say at Work – But Are Actually Racist, Sexist or Offensive."

[223] Sandberg, *Lean In,* 79.

Sexual Behaviors and Why This Bonds Men and Women

[224]Samantha Schmidt, "Beyond 'No Means No': What Most Parents Are Not Teaching their Sons about Sex," *The Washington Post*, published October 4, 2018, accessed April

14, 2020, https://www.washingtonpost.com/local/ social-issues/beyond-no-means-no-how-to-talk-to-teenage-boys-about-sexual-consent/2018.

[225] Kate Julian, "Why Are Young People Having So Little Sex?," *The Atlantic*, published December 2018, accessed April 14, 2020, https://www.theatlantic.com/magazine/archive/2018/12/the-sex-recession/573949/.

[226] Kate Julian, "Why Are Young People Having So Little Sex?"

[227] Ibid.

[228] Centers for Disease Control, "Fewer High School Students Having Sex, Using Drugs," *CDC*, published June 14, 2018, accessed April 14, 2020, https://www.cdc.gov/media/releases/2018/p0614-yrbs.html.

[229] Wikipedia, "iGen," *Wikipedia*, published 2017, accessed April 14, 2020, https://en.wikipedia.org/wiki/ IGen_(book).

[230] Wikipedia, "iGen.".

[231] Kara Mayer Robinson, "10 Surprising Health Benefits of Sex," *WebMD*, updated 2020, accessed April 14, 2020, https://www.webmd.com/sex-relationships/guide/sex-and-health#1.

[232] Dr. David Weeks and Jamie James, "Sex 'Key' to Staying Young," *BBC News*, published October 10, 2000, accessed April 17, 2020, http://news.bbc.co.uk/2/hi/uk_news/scotland/965045.stm.

[233] Ben's Natural Health Team, "Frequent Ejaculation May Reduce Prostate Cancer Risk," *Ben's Natural Health*, published May 30, 2019, accessed April 17, 2020, https://www.bensnaturalhealth.com/blog/masturbation-and-prostate-cancer/.

[234] Cure Joy Editorial, "Can Sex Relieve Migraine Headaches?" *Advizz Me*, published March 6, 2018, accessed April 17, 2020, https://www.advizz.me/content/can-sex-relieve-migraine-headaches/amp/.

[235] A. Hambach, S. Evers, O. Summ, et al., "The Impact of Sexual Activity on Idiopathic Headaches: An Observational Study," *NCBI*, published February 19, 2013, accessed April 17, 2020, https://www.ncbi.nlm.nih.gov/pubmed/23430983.

236 Dr. Hui Liu and Linda Waite, "Bad Marriage, Broken Heart?" *Science Daily*, published November 19, 2014, accessed April 17, 2020, https://www.sciencedaily.com/releases/2014/11/141119204855.htm.

237 Jessica Wood, Serge Desmarais, Tyler Burleigh, and Robin Milhausen, "Reasons for Sex and Relational Outcomes in Consensually Nonmonogamous and Monogamous Relationships," *Journal of Science and Personal Relationships*, 2018; 35 (4): 632.

238 Jessica Wood, Serge Desmarais, Tyler Burleigh, and Robin Milhausen, "Reasons for Sex and Relational Outcomes in Consensually Nonmonogamous and Monogamous Relationships."

239 Ibid.

240 Benjamin Franklin, "Ben Franklin about Wisdom, Life, Age," *Wise Quote*, accessed May 24, 2020. https:// wise-quote.com/Benjamin-Franklin.

For A Better Marriage Act Like a Single Person

241 Ibn Taymiyyah, "Find and Share Quotes with Friends," *Goodreads*, accessed September 9, 2019, https://

www.goodreads.com/quotes/646901-don-t-depend-too-much-on-anyone-in-this-world-because.

242 Stephanie Coontz, "For a Better Marriage, Act Like a Single Person," *The New York Times*, published February 10, 2018, accessed September 9, 2019, https://www.nytimes.com/2018/02/10/opinion /sunday/for-a-better-marriage-act-like-a-single-person.html.

243 Stephanie Coontz, "For a Better Marriage, Act like a Single Person."

244 Ashley Mateo, "The Surprising Benefits of Being Single," *The Oprah Magazine*, published June 10, 2019, accessed September 6, 2019, https://www.oprahmag.com/life/relationships-love/a27790346/benefits-of-being-single/.

245 Julian Holt-Lunstad, Timothy B. Smith and J. Bradley Layton, "Social Relationships and Mortality Risk: A Meta- analytic Review," *PLOS/Medicine (Public Library of Science)*, published July 27, 2010, accessed September 10, 2019, https://journals.plos.org/plosmedicine/article?id=10.1371/journal.pmed.1000316.

246 Harper Lee, "Find and Share Quotes with Friends," *Goodreads,* accessed September 10, 2019, https://www.goodreads.com/quotes/138836-you-can-choose-your-friends-but-you-sho-can-t-choose.

247 Cecilia Dey, "Looking at Things from a Different Angle," *Picture This*, published April 8, 2014, accessed November 3, 2019,

https://ceciliadeyprevails.wordpress.com/2014/04/08/family-is-not-about-blood-its-about-who-is-willing-to-hold-your-hand-when-you-need-it-the-most/.

248 Elyakim Kislev, "The Impacts of Friendship on Single and Married People," *Psychology Today*, posted April 7, 2019, accessed September 11, 2019, https://www.psychologytoday.com/us/blog/happy-singlehood/201904/the- impact-friendships-single-and-married-people.

249 William Chopik and Andy Henion, "Are Friends Better for Us Than Family," *Michigan State University Today*, published June 6, 2017, accessed September 11, 2019, https://msutoday.msu.edu/news/2017/are-friends-better-for- us-than-family/.

[250] Pure Love Quotes, "Quote by Anonymous," *Pure Love Quotes*, published 2019, accessed November 3, 2019, https://www.purelovequotes.com/author/anonymous/one-smile-can-start-a-friendship-one-word-can/.

Friends with Benefits

[251] Harmeet Kaur, "A Landmark Study Shows What Makes a Successful Relationship," *CNN*, published July 29, 2020, accessed September 3, 2020, https://baltimore.cbslocal.com/2020/07/29/a-landmark-study-shows-what-makes-a-successful-relationship/.

Why Men Stay Single?

[252] Mario Abad, "The 43 Most Common Reasons Why Men Stay Single," *Men's Health*, published August 9, 2018, accessed May 24, 2020, https://www.menshealth.com/trending-news/a22685869/single-men-reddit-study//.

[253] The Economic Times India, "Five Benefits of Dating a Smart Woman," *The Economic Times India*, published December 18, 2015, accessed August 7, 2020, https://economictimes.indiatimes.com/magazines/panache/five-benefits-of-dating-a-smart-woman/articleshow/50227030.cms?from=mdr.

254 Robinson Meyer, "Dude, She's (Exactly 25%) Out of Your League," *The Atlantic*, published August 10, 2018, accessed May 24, 2020, https://www.theatlantic.com/science/archive/2018/08/online-dating-out-of-your-league/ 567083/.

255 Elizabeth Bruch and Mark Neuman, "A New Paper by Complex Systems Professors Elizabeth Burch and Mark Neuman Describes a Large-Scale Study of Online Dating Behavior," *LSA Complex Systems University of Michigan*, published August 14, 2028, accessed May 24, 2020, https://lsa.umich.edu/cscs/news-events/all-news/search-news/ elizabeth-bruch--mark-newman-online-dating-research-paper-gains-.html.

256 Elizabeth Bruch and Mark Neuman, "A New Paper by Complex Systems Professors Elizabeth Burch and Mark Neuman Describes a Large-Scale Study of Online Dating Behavior."

257 Deborah Carr and Kathrin Boerner, "Do Spousal Discrepancies in Marital Quality Assessments Affect Psychological Adjustment to Widowhood?," *Journal of Marriage and Family*, 71, no. 1, February 2009, 495-509, accessed May 24, 2020, http://sites.bu.edu/deborahcarr/files/2018/01/carrboerner_jmf_2 009.pdf.

[258] André Aciman, "André Aciman Quotes," *Goodreads*, updated 2020, accessed December 1, 2020, https://www.goodreads.com/quotes/10056606-some-people-may-be-brokenhearted-not-because-they-ve-been-hurt#.

Hope for Women and Society

[259] United States Census Bureau, "Data: Selected Social Characteristics in the United States – American Community Survey 2016," United States Census Bureau, published 2016, accessed May 24, 2020, https://data.census.gov/cedsci/table?d=ACS%205-Year%20Estimates%20Data%20Profiles&table=DP02&tid=ACSDP5Y2016.DP02.

[260] United States Census Bureau, "Data: Selected Social Characteristics in the United States – American Community Survey 2016.

[261] U.S. Bureau of Labor Statistics, "Economic News Release: Employment Characteristics of Families Summary," *U.S. Bureau of Labor Statistics*, published April 21, 2020, accessed May 24, 2020, https://www.bls.gov/news.release/famee.nr0.htm.

[262] U.S. Bureau of Labor Statistics, "Economic News Release: Employment Characteristics of Families Summary."

[263] LEAN IN- Sheryl Sandberg, Pages 104-121, "Make Your Partner a Real Partner".

[264] Ravi Soni, "Relations are like electric currents...," *Your Quote*, published August 3, 2017, accessed May 24, 2020, https://www.yourquote.in/ravi-soni-c24h/quotes/relation-s-like-electric-current-wrong-connection-give- you-s-91rf.

[265] Abby Schultz, "The Wealthy Will Transfer $15.4 Trillion by 2030," *Barrons*, published June 26, 2019, accessed May 24, 2020, https://www.barrons.com/articles/the-wealthy-will-transfer-15-4-trillion-by-2030-01561574217.

[266] Anatole France, "All changes, even the most longed for...," *Goodreads*, published June 27, 2015, accessed May 24, 2020, https://www.goodreads.com/quotes/15645-all-changes-even-the-most-longed-for-have-their-melancholy.

[267] Buddha's Teaching & Science, "Relationships Are Not Exams to Pass...," *Google Buddha Teachings*, published October 14, 2019, accessed May 24, 2020, https://www.google.com/search?%20source=univ&tbm=isch&q=Relationships+are.

[268] James Hamblin, "Evidence of the Superiority of Female Doctors: New Research Estimates That If All Physicians Were Female, 32,000 Fewer Americans Would Die

Every Year," *The Atlantic*, published December 19, 2016, accessed May 24, 2020, https://www.theatlantic.com/health/archive/2016/12/female-doctors-superiority/511034/.

[269] Author Unknown, "Always try to have eyes…," *Quotespedia*, updated 2020, accessed December 1, 2020, https://www.quotespedia.org/authors/u/unknown/always-pray-to-have-eyes-that-see-the-best-a-heart-that-forgives-the-worst-a-mind-that-forgets-the-bad-and-a-soul-that-never-loses-faith-in-god-unknown/.

Last Thoughts to Ponder

[270] Leah Fessler, "MacArthur Genius Ai-jen Poo Makes the Economic Case for Listening," *Quartz at Work*, published February 6, 2018, accessed May 25, 2020, https://qz.com/work/1185580/national-domestic-workers-alliance-director-ai-jen-poo-makes-the-economic-case-for-listening/.

[271] Compassion and the Individual | The 14th Dalai Lama,https://www.dalailama.com/messages/compassion-and-human-values/compassion.

[272] Leah Fessler, "Yale Astrophysicist Priyamvada Natarajan on Mansplaining: It's Just Too Boring," *Quartz at*

Work, published February 6, 2018, accessed May 25, 2020, https://qz.com/work/1176791/yale-astrophysicist-priyamvada-natarajan-wants-you-to-quit-the-mansplaining-its-just-too-boring/.

273 John Naisbitt, "The most exciting breakthroughs of the 21st century...," *Quote Fancy*, published 2020, accessed May 25, 2020, https://quotefancy.com/quote/1340364/John-Naisbitt-The-most-exciting-breakthroughs-of-the-21st-century-will-not-occur-because.

274 Ralph Waldo Emerson, "Success," *Word Press*, updated 2020, accessed May 29, 2020, *Ralph Waldo Emerson Images,* https://ralphwaldoemersonimages.wordpress.com/emerson-ephemera/ success/.

About the Author

Dr. Patel's family's journey and her personal experiences from India to Africa to the United Kingdom transformed her into a global citizen. She came to live in America at the age of 26 years, at which time she embraced being an American. She has been passionate about the basic tenets of personal responsibility, respect and integrity of oneself and neighbor, community spirit and participation, a just and fair work environment, the institution of government for all people, and a final exit at the end of life, leaving behind a positive legacy.

As a licensed, practicing psychiatrist with over 25 years of experience working with both children and adults, her area of expertise focused on her patients' acceptance of their trauma and with her assistance and ability to enable them to heal and restore their well-being. She believes in strong relationships, be it with yourself, your partner, children, parents, or friends. Because of her training, she hopes to provide guidance about healthy male/female relationships and parenting issues.

She feels it is imperative for all Americans to recognize societal ills, take responsibility for healing themselves and change the destiny of American life for future generations.

Dr. Shila Patel, M.D.

Note from the Author

When I first started writing this book, I was mainly interested in exploring the ramifications of the #MeToo Movement and the impact of school shootings in the United States. These topics dominated the media in 2018. As time passed, I felt compelled to write about other societal issues. After finishing the book, it included so much information that I needed to divide the book into two books: the first, exploring relationships as a couple or a family unit; the second, examining societal issues and the all-encompassing Covid-19 pandemic of 2020.

Presently I am contemplating a third book based on the fracture of American society beginning with the events of January 6th, 2021, the rioting and insurrection at the Capital Building in Washington D.C., loss of freedom for women in what they can and cannot do with their own bodies, multiple issues involving the vaccinated and the unvaccinated citizens of the US, and mental health. Politicians continue to pander to their party affiliates instead of taking care of the needs of all their constituents. We are in the throes of a cultural collapse of our society. Self-destructive behavior, irrational thinking, and general mistrust of all authoritative figures have infiltrated every facet of our daily lives. It is only with an in-depth analysis and discussion of these issues that we can restore our beliefs in what it means to be an American citizen living in the United States of America.

Word-of-mouth is crucial for any author to succeed. If you enjoyed reading *Us Unhinged*, please leave a review on the webpage or email at usunhinged@gmail.com. Your comments will be very much appreciated.

Thank you!

Dr. Shila Patel, M.D.

CPSIA information can be obtained
at www.ICGtesting.com
Printed in the USA
BVHW031958301121
622895BV00006B/121